Gender Affirming Therapy

T0368851

Gender Affirming Therapy

A guide to what transgender and non-binary clients can teach us

Laura Scarrone Bonhomme,
Skye Davies and Dr Michael Beattie

 Open University Press

Open University Press
McGraw Hill
Unit 4,
Foundation Park
Roxborough Way
Maidenhead
SL6 3UD

email: emea_uk_ireland@mheducation.com
world wide web: www.openup.co.uk

First edition published 2023

A catalogue record of this book is available from the British Library

ISBN-13: 978-0-3352-5154-4
ISBN-10: 0335251544
eISBN: 978-0-3352-5155-1

Library of Congress Cataloging-in-Publication Data
CIP data applied for

Typeset by Transforma Pvt. Ltd., Chennai, India

Praise Page

"This book is a hugely important and accessibly written, practical resource that demystifies a range of socially-created challenges that diverse, multidimensional trans- and non-binary people have to face from in/visibility and scrutiny, religious belief/hostility, and everyday relationships to sexuality. Based on accounts of experience of trans and non-binary people, and written by practitioners who are especially well-placed to advise, including one non-binary author, the book is compulsory reading for anyone, personally and/or professionally, seeking to support trans and non-binary individuals and community groups. Its reflective focus is vital for anyone wishing to create a more diverse and inclusive world."

Dr Paul Simpson, Lecturer in Sociology, University of Manchester, UK
and extensively published in gender and sexuality in later life

"This book is a welcome and much needed resource on Gender Affirmative Therapy to guide therapists and practitioners to ensure best clinical practices when working with gender. It is a lucid, highly accessible and comprehensive manual that is both thoughtful and thought provoking in emphasising points of reflection that engages the reader in reflexivity and how to integrate practical skills into their therapeutic thinking, formulation and practice. I highly commend the authors wisdom and approach and believe that this book provides an indispensable addition to any practitioners bookshelf."

Christiane Sanderson, Independent Counsellor, London, UK

"There are insights here. I welcome this book because it reminds therapists to engage deeply in reflexive interrogation of clinical privilege, and to centre the narratives and wisdom of the trans and non-binary people we serve. More of that please!"

Matthew Mills (he, him), President of the British Association
of Gender Identity Specialists, Lead Consultant Speech and
Language Therapist, writer, pedagogue and queer activist

Contents

For further resources, including video content, worksheets and others, please visit: www.affirm.lgbt

Contributors

Laura Scarrone Bonhomme is an HCPC-registered Consultant Clinical Psychologist. She trained and developed her career internationally, working in Spain, Chile and the UK. Laura specialises in Gender, Sexual and Relationship Diversity; she frequently delivers psychotherapy, supervision, assessment and training in this area, and has quantitative and theoretical publications in this field. Laura is part of the HM Courts & Tribunals Service List of Specialists in the Field of Gender Dysphoria and of the Gender Diversity Specialist Register of the BPS. She is a Member of the British Association of Gender Identity Specialists and a member of World Professional Association for Transgender Health.

Skye Davies is currently studying a Postgraduate Diploma in Counselling and Psychotherapy at the University of East London. They are employed as a Peer Support Worker at TransPlus, the Adult Gender Dysphoria Clinic based at 56 Dean Street under the Chelsea and Westminster NHS Trust. Skye is also a Volunteer Counsellor at Metro where they work with LGBTQ+ people. They previously worked as an Assistant Psychologist at the Tavistock and Portman NHS Adult Gender Dysphoria Clinic. Skye is a member of the British Association of Gender Identity Specialists and the British Association of Counselling and Psychotherapy.

Dr Michael Beattie is an HCPC-Registered Chartered Counselling Psychologist with a research interest in the psychology of men and masculinities. He has a BSc in Psychology and Counselling and a PsychD in Counselling Psychology, both from Roehampton University. He has worked in the field of sexuality, sexual identity and sexual health as well as with issues of gender identity and gender dysphoria at the NHS Gender Identity Clinic in London. His book *Counselling Skills for Working with Gender Diversity and Identity* was published with colleagues by Jessica Kingsley in 2018. He currently works as a Counselling Psychologist in private practice and provides training and CPD to mental health professionals in the areas of gender, gender identity and sexuality. Prior to entering the field of counselling psychology Michael worked in marketing communications, facilitating strategic planning and training sessions for clients across the world.

Foreword

I am sitting at my computer trying to finish writing this foreword. It's only a few more words yet it is hard to focus, not just because of brain fog but because there has been yet another shooting at a queer club in the US. The repeated heartbreak at the ongoing violence towards queer and trans people right now is loud and insistent. It makes it hard to find a pathway through words. You might wonder why this is relevant in a foreword for a book on gender-affirming care, especially one focused on the UK, although it has content that can benefit mental health providers anywhere.

Misinformation and even malicious messaging about gender-affirming care abound right now, both in the US and the UK. We can debate whether it is ignorance or malice but, given that life is not binary, I would vote for both. The reality is that the spread of inaccurate and even false information is increasing the level of violence both at individualised and systemic levels towards trans, non-binary and/or gender expansive people. Words fan the flames of action, as any political leader and movement organiser knows. If the messaging is that 'our children are at risk' from trans and queer people and that 'gender-affirming care is part of the trans agenda', I am sadly not surprised that some people are taking it upon themselves to make sure that gender-affirming care is not available to anyone and, in some extreme cases, are even moved to violence towards us.

This is why books like this one are so important. Authors and clinicians Laura, Skye and Michael guide the reader through the 'world of gender' and across the many possible pathways that you might encounter when working with trans, non-binary and/or gender expansive clients from a gender-affirming perspective. They walk the fine line between navigating the medicalised world of mental health and valuing the lived experiences of their clients, as well as their own. The pathways on the journey are numerous and they kindly signpost essential moments for reflection throughout their writing. While reading this book, I appreciated the transparency of their approach and their desire to give space to the experiences of trans, non-binary and gender expansive people. If you are feeling lost or alone as a provider when navigating gender-affirming care, I believe this book can be a friend to you and guide you to a place of knowledge and connection. As the world around us continues to be at times inhospitable for many of us who are trans, non-binary, gender expansive and/or queer, I appreciate this contribution to building a more welcoming 'world of gender' for us all.

Alex Iantaffi, PhD, MS, CST, SEP, LMFT

Author of *Gender Trauma: Healing Cultural, Social, and Historical Gendered Trauma*

Preface

I am sitting in my west London office surrounded by half-living plants and, honestly, feeling slightly embarrassed by them. I worry about my clients inferring any meaning from their balding stems, in particular about my 'caring abilities'. You see, my problem is that sometimes I cannot resist overwatering them; to give them just a little bit more, just in case. The poor plants end up flooding. Only now I question if this echoes my inclinations as a therapist. It is hard to know how much to give. You have to listen for long enough so that the client owns the space, but not for so long that you would seem disengaged. You have to offer guidance, without being overbearing. You have to ask questions, but only when the client is ready to explore the answers. You have to be a real person, without disclosing too much about yourself. The emotional contortionism that is therapy requires us to constantly measure the temperature in the room, mirroring our clients enough so that they feel seen, yet challenged. I have always felt that therapy is a lot like comedy: it is all about the timing, the tone and knowing your audience. As much as it is tremendously rewarding, therapy can be exhausting for all parties involved. My back knows it very well and, on occasions, my body seems more engaged than my brain. Sometimes, my neck complains from intensely tilting my head, like a dog trying to make sense of 'human words'. It is undeniable that our bodies pay the price of juggling equilibrium for our clients, of creating this artificial womb where others can get reacquainted with their vulnerabilities.

There is something cathartic about this writing, about being able to use 'I', when we have been trained to talk so cautiously. It is not often enough that, as therapists, we are allowed to share the inner workings of our brains. There are few safe spaces where we are allowed to reveal what happens on this side of the therapy room, like in supervision or seminars. Before the start of the pandemic, I used to cherish travelling to north London to partake in these gatherings. For anyone who is not familiar with the scenery, London holds this appeal of psychodynamic tradition; there, standing proud, are the Freud Museum, the Anna Freud Centre, and the Tavistock and Portman. Hampstead efficiently delivers on the archetypes of the city, with grand Victorian bleached white houses and leafy walks. Also, it is the Mecca to many psychotherapists who go on pilgrimage to visit Freud's couch. You don't have to wait long to stumble across groups of bohemian women in power necklaces and statement spectacles. A friend once told me, if you lift a stone anywhere in north London, flocks of psychotherapists will come out startled. It made me laugh.

In the absence of these spaces, where perhaps would we meet, sit side by side and ask, 'Where do you work? What do you specialise in? And, by chance, do we have a common acquaintance?' I would like to draw you in for us to have a chat over coffee, tea or, for my compatriot South Americans, a shared *mate.*

Like in therapy, I would like to be a real person with you without making this book too much about myself, but about what it has been like to work with clients who identify as transgender, trans, non-binary, genderqueer, gender-diverse, gender expansive, or simply 'not cis'. I would like to bring the focus to the stories they have told me and, to protect their identities, I will change some details to ensure that the essence of the learning is there. So, like in cinematographic productions, allow me to use the disclaimer that *this book is based on a true story*.

Why should you read this book?

Perhaps it is a bit too late to make a point about it, given that, if you are reading this, you have purchased and are holding this book. That's a pound in my pocket and, with a smirk on my face, I am almost tempted to dust my hands in a satisfied manner, 'Good job, Laura, your work here is done.' But I would be lying to myself. I would hope that you would take at least one thing away from this reading: something that you have learned about others, or something that you have learned about yourself. So, tell me, what brought you here?

I'll tell you how I landed in the field of gender, sexual and relationship diversity. And I say 'landed' because, apart from having watched a few documentaries and movies, I had never met a transgender or non-binary person before in the flesh. Many of my closest friends identify as gay, bi, or queer, but, as I soon enough learned, it is not at all the same thing. One lucky morning, I came across a job advert looking for a clinical psychologist to work in 'the largest and oldest Gender Identity Clinic in the world'. And, aside from this flashy sentence, there is not much more to the story than that I miraculously got the job.

For the longest time, I worked with general mental health, young people and families, with psychiatric conditions, with physical illnesses, but I was frequently dissatisfied by how we continued to split humans in half. There is the mind and there is the body. And no one seems to realise that they are essentially the same thing! Our training as psychological practitioners and that of medics is ridiculously split and so, to me, gender represented a haven to practise actual integration. Not only between body and mind, but also with identity, society, law, history and every aspect of what makes you 'you'. I did not know this at the time, and I mostly compensated for my lack of familiarity with the issues pertinent to this field with curiosity. I was fascinated by the idea of individuals coming to a crucial point of self-realisation that allowed them to change their lives in ways that others struggled to understand. I was intrigued by the reasoning and the strength required to follow one's truth, particularly when in doing so, stigma and rejection often followed. Most importantly, I wished to know what lessons were to be learned that only transgender and non-binary people could teach us; those that, as a cisgender person, I could not discover on my own. But also, what could I learn about my own gender identity, as this was a question that, before coming into this field, I had neglected to ask.

I guess that what I am saying is, if this is the first time you are taking a closer look at gender diversity issues, there is no shame in it. I can relate to the feeling of intimidation or concern when working in this heavily political area, to the 'Did I say something wrong? What words should I use to ask about this? Gosh, I hope I did not offend him'. The problem with this is that gender issues become tremendously specialised and clients, who are in desperate need of emotional support, become seen as people who can only be supported by experts. Clients do not know whether it is safe to open up and whether they will be judged or encouraged to resolve their issues by digging a hole in the ground and burying them there. Reparative therapy is still used to 'correct' people's differences and so, as a client, 'How would I know if, deep inside, you think that I am a freak?' Hence the need to build a bridge so that therapists feel prepared to support gender-diverse communities in a way that is effective, ethical and affirmative.

What will I find?

You have ahead of you 11 chapters introducing you to each issue that my co-authors and I most frequently encountered in clinical practice and while providing training for healthcare professionals. There are no two cisgender people who are the same, and this also applies to gender-diverse people. So, apologies in advance as it would be impossible for us to collect every single narrative in this book. In terms of how you might approach this reading, I must admit that it is challenging to draw a line in between these issues as many are multi-layered and interconnected, so you will see mention of similar elements within different sections of the book. Aside from that, we recommend that you approach the reading in order.

We will start this journey with *Arriving at the world of gender*, as this chapter sets up the scene of the world of gender and sexual diversity. It describes the history of sex and gender as interlinked constructs, and it normalises the existence of diversity within human experience. You will be supported to challenge inherited preconceptions around LGBTQI+ communities, forming a firm base to deliver affirmative practice. We will note the importance of the use of language, introducing you to relevant terminology. Drawing from scientific evidence, we will describe the demographics and characteristics within gender-diverse communities, with a brief exploration of the high co-occurrence of Autism Spectrum Conditions among these groups.

Dr Michael Beattie will introduce us in Chapter 2 to *Working with identity-based trauma (IBT)*. In this chapter, we will focus on the prevailing social stigma of LGBTQI+ communities and use the concept of IBT to explore what it is like to hold a minority identity. The chapter goes on to explore the impact of aggressions and microaggressions, manifestations of IBT in relation to internalised transphobia and shame, and traditional trauma responses within the body.

In Chapter 3, *Strategies to come out*, we will explore the psychological processes involved in the act of revealing one's gender or sexual identity to others, colloquially referred to as 'coming out'. This is a common psychotherapeutic theme, as clients bring to us their fears of vulnerability, worries of losing their families, seeking support and reassurance on how to best approach the conversation. To work with these issues, we will present practical steps and considerations.

Clients are sometimes confronted with uncertainty around transition and de-transition. In Chapter 4, *Arriving at the right decision*, we will explore the surgical and hormonal interventions that gender-diverse people undergo to achieve congruence. Aiming to provide you with sufficient knowledge to support client's informed decisions, we will consider the challenges of guiding individuals who do not express a heightened degree of dysphoria, nor euphoria, and for whom stepping away from their known reality can be particularly challenging.

In Chapter 5, *Beyond the gender binary*, Skye Davies explores what it means to identify outside of the gender binary of man or woman. We will consider the gender binary in its social and historical context and how language has evolved along with our understanding of non-binary identities. We will explore what it means for non-binary people to realise their unique gender expression, body configuration, and ways of relating to the world. We will debunk some of the common misconceptions around non-binary people and illustrate how their specific struggles may show up in therapy.

Chapter 6, *What about the parents?*, will concentrate on the experience of parents of trans and non-binary people, since this commonly neglected group frequently struggles to understand their children's identity and desire to transition. It is common for parents to be confronted with feelings of loss, confusion and fear that get in the middle of accepting their adult children. Therefore, this chapter offers activities to support the processing of these emotions and repair family dynamics.

In Chapter 7, *Sexuality, romance and identity labels*, we will consider how the reconfiguration of trans people's bodies, experiences of sexual pleasure, intimacy and other factors become a key part of a couple's concerns around the survival of their relationship through and following transition. When a trans or non-binary person comes out, this pushes their significant other/s to consider a number of elements about their relationship, as well as themselves. Many partners examine their own gender, sexual identity labels and belonging to queer or straight communities. In this chapter we will take into consideration how to negotiate these changes.

Many religions have depicted gender and sexually diverse individuals as immoral or anomalous. In Chapter 8, *What would God say?*, we will address the internal conflict experienced by gender-diverse people who have been raised in a particular faith and for whom, in being trans, their spirituality and connection to their communities is at stake. In this chapter we will explore the reasons why trans people might struggle to reconcile their beliefs with their identity, we will introduce a client's experiences of reparative praying and provide strategies to help our clients find peace within themselves.

Cisgender, trans, and non-binary people might struggle with body image and, by extension, with looking in the mirror. In an image-focused society like the one we live in, looks can get confused with a person's overall value. In Chapter 9, *Clients' relationship with the mirror*, we will consider the relational patterns that gender-diverse folk form with the mirror and will provide strategies to ensure healthier dynamics of self-relation.

Chapter 10, *What if they clock me?*, addresses clients' fears of being identified as gender-diverse, what is commonly known as being 'clocked'. We will explore the meaning of these concerns and describe the broad differences between transmasculine, transfeminine and non-binary people. We will address strategies to nourish self-acceptance and confidence to manage situations in which one's trans status might be recognised by others. We will also support clients to assess safety and consider appropriate courses of action.

Chapter 11, *Digital tools and online identities*, reflects upon the scenarios where delivering telephone and video-conference sessions might be particularly suited to support individuals who experience dysphoria. Also, we will examine the importance and function of online communities for trans and non-binary folk, as well as their digital self-portrayal.

Lastly, as we wished to bring the voices of the communities into this book without filtering them through the lens of practitioners, Skye Davies has interviewed trans and non-binary individuals on a variety of relevant themes, such as de-transition, access to psychotherapy, sex and dating, and so on. We also invited a group of parents of trans people to speak about their experiences. These interviews were transcribed and edited, in collaboration with the interviewees, and can be found at the end of some of the chapters under the title 'In their own words'. We have used either first names or pseudonyms to identify the interviewees, according to their preferences.

For further resources, including video content, worksheets and others, please visit: www.affirm.lgbt

Acknowledgement and intentions

This is a work of dedication to our beloved clients, those who we have seen shine over the course of therapy and those who are still trying to find their way. They are our mentors and our informers. Also, thank you to the interviewees who generously volunteered their time and experiences; their voices are crucial to this book.

Fox Fisher (foxfisher.com) is an award-winning graphic designer, illustrator and gif creator with an LGBTQIA+ focus, who has designed for many LGBTQIA+ organisations. Their work has included logos, promotional material, or creative content for brands, organisations and companies. We are delighted to have worked with them to create our unique and beautiful cover art and want to thank them for the contribution they have made to your experience and enjoyment of the book.

Dr Alex Iantaffi (alexiantaffi.com) is an author, independent scholar, licensed marriage and family therapist, with over 20 years' experience in contributing to the literature on Deafness, disability, HIV, gender, sexuality, relationships and trauma with an extensive body of work in peer-reviewed journal articles, books and book chapters. As an influential voice in the LGBTQIA+ field, they are perfectly placed to introduce you to our book, and we are especially thankful to them for the time they have taken to read our manuscript and write the Foreword.

From Laura Scarrone Bonhomme

I am an able-bodied, heterosexual and cisgender woman and my pronouns are She/her. I was born in Spain, but my ethnicity is not straightforward. I fall somewhere between European, South American, and who knows what other love affairs. I come from a long lineage of emigrants and, maybe being destined to it, I became one myself. I know what it is like to struggle economically. English is my second language and, like most people, I sit somewhere between the structures of privilege and oppression. I do not have a lived experience of gender dysphoria, nor do I know first-hand what is like to live outside the high walls of heteronormativity. I have tried to convey to the best of my abilities what clients have relayed to me over thousands of hours of spoken and silent exchanges. I can only hope not to have misrepresented the communities, nor to have excluded anyone with my language or my manner. I can only reassure you of my intention to be an accomplice to this cause.

From Skye Davies

I am a transfeminine non-binary person, and my pronouns are she/they. I entered the world of trans healthcare in 2018 as an Assistant Psychologist at the Tavistock and Portman NHS Adult Gender Dysphoria Clinic where I worked for three years. It was here that I met my co-authors, Laura and Michael, and developed my understanding of the field. The intersection of my trans identity with other aspects of my identity (such as being white, middle class, non-disabled) means that I speak from a place of relative social privilege. Therefore, the experiences and struggles of other trans people will be different from my own. I encourage readers to continue their learning by reading the works of others in the community, particularly those who are working class, people of colour, disabled and neurodiverse.

From Michael Beattie

In writing about gender diversity, I feel it is important to situate myself and be explicit about the ways in which my own experience both intersects with and differs from that of my clients.

I am an able-bodied, gay, cisgender man and my pronouns are he/him/his. I started working in the field of trans healthcare when, after some years working in marketing communications, I embarked on a change of career and retrained as a counselling psychologist. I initially took up a placement at the London NHS Adult Gender Dysphoria Clinic in 2010, later returning to the clinic full-time, where I met and worked alongside Laura and Skye. Although I know I have a great deal of privilege through being a middle-class, able-bodied, privately educated, white man, I also have intersectional experience of discrimination and othering through my sexuality. My own male gender role socialisation was pretty harsh and affected by the time and culture I grew up in, suffused as it was by the AIDS panic and Section 28. Initially, I felt like there must be something wrong with me but, after quite a bit of personal therapy and my own psychological training, I began to realise that the problem might instead be the harsh masculine norms I grew up with and that I might not be the only person struggling with and hurt by them. This has driven my ongoing research interest in the psychology of men and masculinities as well as my focus on working with LGBTQI+ clients, which I now do in private practice.

I hope that what I share in these pages, along with my fellow authors, is both representative and inclusive of the experiences of my clients as well as helpful in supporting the reader to connect with the experience of their clients as they navigate and try to make sense of questions of gender identity and diversity.

1 Arriving at the world of gender

What makes a man?

I must admit, I have always been fascinated by Orthodox Judaism. I am not sure what first caught my eye, if it is the uniformed style of clothing or how removed the lives of Orthodox Jews are from mine, but when in 2018 I was given the opportunity to travel to Jerusalem, I jumped at it. I found myself bewildered by their way of navigating the chaotic streets of Jerusalem. I was told that, among other principles, the lives of Orthodox Jewish people are guided by that of 'what one can see, cannot be unseen'. Anything could lead to sinful thoughts and with many foreigners like myself on the streets (wearing shorts and no sleeves) I can only imagine what a psychological minefield that must have been! Preventing harm to the soul, some walked in pairs, one averting the gaze from everything but the pebbles on the road, and another self-sacrificing while leading the way. I now think that they might have been onto something. After working with so many stigmatised groups, I understand how what we repeatedly see and hear eventually becomes part of us.

Wherever you sit in the ideological spectrum, you might want to stop and consider how much of your beliefs are influenced by sources external to you, by the apparently harmless homophobic jokes Uncle Tom told, the TV commercials showcasing cleaning products for dutiful wives, or by the Instagram post that made you reconsider getting Botox. For most of my life I was oblivious to the slow yet eroding effect of these experiences and how, by pure exposure, they lower the bar of what we consider to be normal. Who we are is not only dependent on the life events that piece our story together, but on the socio-political ideas of the era, the religion of our country, the values of our family, the times we were grounded or the shows we watched. Anyone who is mildly interested in the world around them will absorb notions of good and bad, adequacy and inadequacy. This is an adaptative strategy triggered by the innate wish to be loved and to belong, given that being rejected by our 'tribe' makes us more vulnerable to worldly threats (Gilbert, 2009, 2017). To be safely loved and accepted by our social group, we inadvertently commit to playing by the rules.

A moment to self-discover

- In what socio-political context were you born, and what messages did you receive around gender equality or inequality?
- If you were raised within a religion, were men and women expected to behave differently or to abide to different mandates?
- What gender role models did you observe within your family?
- Were you ever reprimanded for expressing yourself in a way that was associated with a different sex from your own?

A little quiz

In your view, which one of the following statements are TRUE or FALSE?

- Women have penises
- Women have moustaches
- Men have wombs and bear children
- Men wear dresses, make-up and pink

These are usually rules that we have not designed ourselves and that we often might not even agree with. Numerous arguments have been presented around what makes a man or a woman and generally these are linked to body, appearance, or interests. Some examples are expressed above, and although you might be able to answer considering a large proportion of the population, the reality is more nuanced than a simple 'true' or 'false'.

Let's examine it. Most people would undoubtedly say that only men have penises so, allow me to ask, under what category would you place a man who in an accident has lost his penis? And would a man without a penis continue to be a man? If your answer is 'yes', then you might have found the first of the reasons that can be presented to support the categorisation of [trans] men (with a vagina and vulva) as men. But, if it is not the penis, then what makes a man? Perhaps it is facial hair, as only men have beards, right? Although, as a Latin woman I can tell you that women can fight their moustaches as much as men do. Globally, between 5 and 20 per cent of women have Polycystic Ovarian Syndrome (PCOS) (Ntumy et al., 2019) a condition that raises natural levels of testosterone increasing women's ability to grow facial and body hair.

People assume that the ability to give birth is reserved to women and for many, it can be a key part of their identity. In reality, there are women who decide not to bear children, experience fertility problems, or are even born without a womb. Would they be less womanly for not fulfilling this biological destiny? Also, there are non-binary and transmasculine people who have a womb and who, at different stages of their transition, have become pregnant.

So, if it is not pregnancy, does being a woman relate to what you wear? Women wear dresses, but so did children (regardless of their gender) up until the end of the Victorian era. Searching on the internet you can find pictures of a young Franklin D. Roosevelt (32nd president of the United States) in a delightful white dress. Ultimately, children just want comfort and what better than a skirt? Pink is the femme colour *par excellence*, even though traditionally it was considered representative of strength and those who wished to signal their manliness wore it. Instead, due to its delicacy, blue was stereotypically feminine, and this pattern was only inverted in the 1940s. For some reason, this fictitious colour coding has become popularised and you will see neatly classified babies, delineated toy stores, and even splashed in pink maternity wards. High heels were designed in the fifteenth century to facilitate men horse-riding, and there are endless examples of how our perception of masculine or feminine presentations vary between countries, cultures and across history. Also, it is not static and so our understanding of what being a man or woman entails constantly evolves, but often we treat these assumptions as fixed parameters to judge one another. So, if your gender is not your genitals, your ability to bear children, nor your moustache or the clothes that we wear, then what the hell is it?

What is sex?

It all started with sex, typically the act of having it that led to your conception, and the sex you were assigned at birth. Our sex is constituted by our chromosomal configuration, the influence of hormones and the environment in our developing brains and bodies. Most people are born with two sets of chromosomes, those with XY are destined to be assigned male and to develop a reproductive system with a penis, scrotum, testes, epididymis, vas deferens, prostate and seminal vesicles. On the other hand, individuals with XX chromosomes are destined to be assigned female and to develop a reproductive system with uterine tubes, uterus, ovary, cervix, vagina, clitoris, the labia majora and labia minora.

The differentiation of our bodies starts in utero. Up until nine weeks of development, foetuses have ambiguous genitals, and by week 12, they have finished differentiating. At 16 weeks, foetuses assigned male (XY) experience a peak in testosterone levels equivalent to that found in adult males. It is amusing to think of a foetus, about, on average, 11.6 cm long, having as much testosterone as the hairiest of men. Between 15 and 24 weeks, female-assigned foetuses (XX) experience a differentiation in their brain structures, in particular the corpus callosum, which is pre-programmed to lose cells. After birth, there are two periods of further differentiation – one at the age of five and the other, most apparent, during puberty. As you may be able to recollect, during puberty, individuals assigned male at birth experience a spurt in testosterone, whereas individuals who are assigned female at birth will see an increase in their oestrogen and progesterone levels causing drastic bodily, social and psychological changes. For more information on these, review Fausto-Sterling (2012).

For a long time, science has tried to find brain differences between males and females – a task that has proven challenging due to difficulty in separating purely biological effects from those caused by the influence of the environment. For example, men and women might display differences in brain structures associated with visual-spatial attitudes, with men broadly showing better aptitudes for this sort of task, however, boys are generally given toys that promote these abilities more frequently than girls. Oftentimes I am asked if there is a test that would help us determine if a person is transgender, and there is no such thing! However, Zhou et al. (1995) studied sexed structural brain differences in the volume of the central subdivision of the Bed nucleus of the Stria Terminalis (BSTc). This is an area that is essential for sexual behaviour and that is not influenced by sex hormones in adulthood (i.e., androgens, oestrogens or progestogens). Broadly, this area is larger in individuals who have been assigned male at birth, than in people assigned female at birth. Zhou and colleagues found an inversion of these patterns in transgender people with a binary identity, with female-sized brain structure in trans women, and a male-sized brain structure in trans men, in accordance with their gender identity, as opposed to their sex.

When were you first pronounced a boy or a girl?

With the development of modern, Western medicine, a new protocol started in maternity wards around the world: the recording of the sex in newborn babies. Currently, using a so-called Phall-O-Meter (Fausto-Sterling, 2000) a healthcare practitioner (often a midwife) examines the baby's genitals to ascertain whether a clitoris or a penis appears present. If the length of the external genitals is shorter than 1.5 cm, it is defined as a clitoris, assigning a female sex. If the length is greater than 3 cm, then it is defined as a penis, and the baby is assigned male. This one letter in your birth certificate (i.e., 'M' or 'F') will guide your life in a number of ways. If you are a boy, you would be expected to like sports, be better at engineering than the average woman, be assertive and sexually attracted to women. This would be instilled in you from an early age, with questions such as 'do you like any girls at school?'. If you are pronounced a girl, then you would be expected to enjoy caring for other people, be obedient and place great importance in your appearance, which will often be reinforced by comments such as 'how delightful you look!'.

So, how did the size of our genitals ever get mixed with all these elements? They are embedded in the notions of *cisnormativity* and *heteronormativity*:

Cisnormativity assumes that everyone in the world (almost 8 billion of us) will either have XX or XY chromosome and that people's gender identity will be expressed within traditional gender stereotypes, matching our birth-assigned sex. This is to say that everyone born with XX chromosomes would develop a female gender identity, and those with XY would have a male gender identity. Cisnormativity disregards the existence of individuals who are transgender, non-binary or gender nonconforming. Not only that, it invalidates the existence of intersex people or those with diversity of sexual development (DSD).

Heteronormativity assumes that individuals assigned male at birth, who develop a male gender identity, will be exclusively attracted to female-assigned people who have a female gender identity. And that the complementary opposite will apply to individuals assigned female at birth, thereby framing heterosexuality and 'opposite-sex' attraction as the only form of sexual orientation. Heteronormativity relies on the binary notion of cisnormativity and disregards the existence of the rich variety of sexual attractions such as lesbian, gay, bisexual, asexual, pansexual and so on.

Cisnormativity and heteronormativity not only are unrealistic, but they restrict everyone in the way in which we are allowed to conceive and express our gender and sexual identities (including that of cisgender and straight people). Can you imagine for a second what would the world be like if we were to remove all these gendered expectations?

Not everything is black or white

Perhaps when reading about the Phall-O-Meter you noticed that there was an unclassified area, that corresponding to individuals whose genitals are sized between 1.5 and 3 cm. They would most commonly fall under the descriptions of intersex or DSD, and this is because not everyone's physiology neatly falls into the categories of female or male. Blackless et al., (2000) established that up to 2 per cent of the population has some form of physiological variance in the expression of their sex chromosome composition, gonadal structure, the structure of the internal genital duct systems and external genitalia and/or hormone levels. However, if we are to purely consider intersex individuals who present with chromosomic differences, and with conditions like: Androgen Insensitivity Syndrome, Congenital Adrenal Hyperplasia, Klinefelter Syndrome, or Turner Syndrome, their prevalence would be much lower at around 0.018 per cent of the general population (Sax, 2002).

So, what influence does cisnormativity have over the healthcare of intersex people or those with DSD? Perhaps we should start by imagining what it would be like to spend nine months awaiting the arrival of your newborn, going through the tiring ordeal of labour and birth and, within hours, being told that your child's genitals are 'deformed'. I can only relate to the concern of any parent, and the desperation to get straight answers from a doctor. Depending on the parent's intellectual and educational background they might even struggle to grasp some of the concepts we have been addressing to fully understand the meaning of this difference. Many doctors may opt for trying to correct what seems to be different and, according to cisnormativity, inherently wrong, creating the kinds of sexed and gendered bodies that heteronormativity demands. Blackless et al. (2000) estimated the frequency of individuals undergoing 'corrective' genital surgery, at between 1 and 2 per 1,000 live births (0.1–0.2 per cent). The issue is that, despite the shape of their genitals, intersex people or those with DSD grow to identify as male, female or non-binary. In taking this rushed decision without the individual's consent and later knowledge of what their identity will be, parents and healthcare professionals determine if the newborn will be raised as either male or female, and some are never told about these surgeries, but only later in life come to experience a sense of incongruence towards their bodies, or to find out that their fertility is compromised.

What is gender?

We constantly encounter gendered experiences, if you are *cisgender* (i.e., your birth assigned sex corresponds with your gender identity) and have never experienced incongruence, perhaps it would escape you how frequently they manifest, but gender-diverse people can encounter daily sources of dysphoria and euphoria. Masculinity, femininity and neutrality live in our bodies and in its sexed characteristics. Prior to puberty and aside from genitalia, boys' and girls' bodies remain mostly undifferentiated, but once puberty strikes with all its smells, fluids and spurts of growth, many struggle to accept these unsolicited and uncontrollable changes. Commonly, trans and non-binary people first become aware of gender incongruence through physical and social pubertal changes which highlight the mismatch with their sense of self.

However, gender is not just about the body, but can also be the place that we occupy in the world. Several components puzzle together our *social gender role*, like the words that people use to refer to us, with the connotations that they carry. For example, being defined as a 'mother' or a 'father' (as opposed to the neutral term 'parent') draws from our mind a set of expectations about the differing responsibilities that society has delineated for each role. Through social conditioning, we associate particular adjectives to each gender, further reinforcing perceived or real differences between men and women. For instance, a woman is more likely to be referred to as 'emotional', whereas a man might be referred to as 'stoic'. For a long time, we have known about the negative impact that these descriptors have in the emotional lives of men, who in order to protect their masculinity, are often socially conditioned to repress emotion. In practical terms, men are less likely to seek mental health support, and more likely to successfully commit suicide than women are (World Health Organization, 2014). Pronouns like 'she/her' or 'he/him' continue to carry unconscious biases around what it inherently means to be male or female, and titles like 'Mrs' and 'Miss' refer to married or unmarried women, establishing if they belong to someone else, whereas these standards have never applied to men (solely using 'Mr').

When passers-by look at you, within a split second they will make a judgement as to whether you are a man or a woman, determining what sort of words, manners and customs apply when addressing you. The way in which others perceive your gender is partially controlled by your *gender presentation*. This is to say the kind of clothes, jewellery, makeup, hairstyle and any other elements that denote femininity, masculinity or neutrality. However, as we previously saw, gender presentation is not static but evolving.

Gender is the way in which we identify in terms of masculinity, femininity, neutrality or a combination of these. Your *internal sense of gender* is composed of feelings towards your body, appearance and other people's perception of you. These feelings elicit congruency or incongruency, reinforcing a true sense of self, or that of alienation. However, let's not omit that cisgender people can also experience discomfort towards gendered features of their bodies and towards societal expectations around their gender. For instance, breast augmentation surgery is one of the most common surgical interventions undergone by women, allowing them to meet societal standards of femininity. Likewise, with the purpose of enhancing their virility, some men seek to have hair transplants. Also, not everyone presents in a quintessential feminine or masculine role, as one can be a feminine woman, tomboy or butch, therefore not complying with traditional expectations of what a woman sounds like, dresses like or enjoys doing.

A moment to self-discover

What is your earliest recollection of becoming aware of your gender? Some people talk about having seen the differences in the anatomy of a sibling or having been placed in a single-sex school. Others firstly realised their sexual identity and through that (based on heteronormative values) understand their gender (i.e., 'I like boys and so I must be a girl').

On gender diversity

Evidently, sex does not always correlate with gender identity and a recent systematic review established that between 0.5 and 4.5 per cent of adults are transgender or gender-diverse (Zhang et al., 2020). Over time, we have observed a gradual increase in the number of people who identify as trans and/or non-binary. It is believed that this evolution is influenced by the de-criminalisation and de-stigmatisation of sexual and gender diversity, which has allowed for greater inclusiveness, protection and visibility of individuals belonging to these communities (Bockting et al., 2016; Stroumsa, 2014).

Within gender-diverse groups, most people continue to identify within a binary frame, Koehler et al. (2018) established that approximately 80 per cent of trans people have a binary gender identity, whereas 20 per cent are non-binary. Individuals with a binary identity, use labels like [trans] man, [trans] woman, transmasculine, or transfeminine. They might want to have a cisnormative body – this is to say the body configuration of a cisgender female or male person – or they might be accepting and secure with a more non-normative body configuration, not desiring to seek surgical interventions. For example, a trans woman with an unequivocal female identity might retain her penis as it does not cause her dysphoria. Also, we might find that trans binary people present in non-traditional gendered ways, for example, a trans man can identify with his femininity (as some cisgender men do) and can present in colourful and flamboyant clothing. The fact that a person is trans does not mean that they ought to present in a heteronormatively feminine or masculine manner, but, like any cisgender person, they will explore and express their identity in myriad ways. Traditionally, there was a higher prevalence of 'medically diagnosed' trans women, mostly because for many people the thought that a person assigned female at birth could transition into a male role seemed inconceivable. Nevertheless, trans men have always existed, even if they did not always come forward for medical interventions to support their transition. Now, however, with the increased visibility of trans men and non-binary transmasculine people, the proportionate imbalance is less evident.

Non-binary (or gender non-conforming) people partially or fully reject traditional conceptualisations of gender, frequently those which have been associated with their birth-assigned sex and which tend to be sources of dysphoria. Interestingly, non-binary identities are more prevalent in individuals assigned female at birth (AFAB). Community and clinical samples seem to agree that on average, two-thirds of non-binary people are AFAB, whereas one-third are assigned male at birth (AMAB) (Arcelus et al., 2016; Koehler et al., 2018). Additionally, in a study my colleagues and I carried out at the London NHS Gender Identity Clinic (formerly known as Charing Cross), we found differences in the use of gender identity labels between female and male assigned non-binary individuals, as a higher proportion of people AMAB identified as non-binary transfeminine (51.1 per cent vs 0.7 per cent [AFAB]); whereas a higher proportion of people AFAB identified as non-binary transmasculine (63.4 per cent vs 2.1 per cent [AMAB]) (Evans et al., 2019). Within this sample, we observed binary tendencies within non-binary groups.

Non-binary communities use a broad variety of umbrella terms to describe their nuanced sense of self. Some individuals self-define as 'agender' and might not identify with either masculine or feminine traits; others describe a fluid sense of their identity which may shift between masculinity and femininity, self-defining as 'genderfluid'; and some may partially identify with femininity and use labels such as 'demi-girl' or 'transfeminine'. Many non-binary people use binary pronouns (i.e., 'she/her', and 'he/him') neutral pronouns (i.e. 'they/them') and/or 'neo-pronouns' like: 'zhe/zhem', 'sie, hir' and so on. Most would feel more congruent with the use of neutral language (like parent, child, partner, etc.) There is a lot more to non-binary identities, and so I will let Skye further guide us on this topic in Chapter 5, *Beyond the gender binary*.

Lastly, trans and non-binary are gender identifications which are stable over time, and they are not to be confused with performative identities, such as drag queens, or purely sexualised like 'cross-dressing' can be. Beware that these terms could be offensive to trans and non-binary people and so always make sure that you are affirmative in the way you refer to your client's identity, using the words and pronouns they choose.

On gender dysphoria

Gender dysphoria refers to the incongruence and/or distress towards the mismatch that exists between a person's gender identity, sexed body and social gender role. Individuals experience varying degrees of dysphoria which can be triggered while on their own and/or around other people. Some feel less incongruent when alone as they can manage the triggers of dysphoria without the unpredictability of how others will perceive them. Take the example of Angie, a non-binary transfeminine person who was assigned male at birth, and who uses 'they/them', as well as 'she/her' pronouns. Angie often feels dysphoric towards her [flat] chest, and among many others, dysphoria might be manifested in feelings of disgust, confusion or helplessness. In order to manage these feelings, she uses prosthetic breasts and padded bras, avoids looking down and wears baggy clothes. The efficiency in the use of these techniques varies from person to person, and is often connected to the degree of dysphoria, the person's ability to bear distress and to accept their reality. For example, Angie might feel very dysphoric towards her chest but, when having thoughts about it, she breathes through the anxiety that it causes her and she reassures herself that soon she will access interventions that will allow her to feel more congruent. In this way, her overall level of dysphoria is manageable. However, consider how different things would be if every time Angie had thoughts about her chest, she would start to think, 'You are disgusting. Nobody would like you with this body.' Also, she would seek to look at her chest to further reinforce these feelings and would not use a padded bra to make herself feel more congruent.

Social dysphoria is closely linked to being *misgendered*, a term that refers to instances when a gender-diverse person is addressed by the name, pronouns and/or title associated to their birth-assigned sex (as opposed to that linked to their gender identity). Trans and non-binary folk can be misgendered by members of the public or people close to them at any point in their transition. This may be more likely to happen at the start, and if they have not yet accessed any gender-affirming interventions, though it is important to remember that many people retain elements associated with their birth-assigned sex even after accessing hormones or surgery. Voice tends to be one of the main elements that could lead a person to misjudge gender, particularly in transfeminine people as voice is not feminised with hormone replacement therapy but through speech and language therapy and practice. Also, non-binary folk are misgendered more often than binary people. They frequently present in non-normative ways and it is still unlikely that members of the public would consider 'they/them' pronouns as an option. After all, we are configured (through the social conditioning inherent in cisnormativity and heteronormativity) to think in binary terms.

As an example, let's consider James, a transmasculine person who was assigned female at birth. James feels particularly triggered when being called 'Ma'am' or referred to as 'she/her'. This is because we tend to think with our bodies as a whole, not just with our brains. By association of ideas, misgendering links words to concepts, feelings and bodily reactions. When James is being called 'Miss', this directs his attention to areas of his presentation that might make others identify him as female. James would wonder, 'Is it my chest?' becoming hyper aware of his chest and the tightness of the binder, experiencing shame, lowering his eyes and disconnecting from the speaker. These interactions could be more, less or equally challenging than encounters with one's anatomy and, in order to avoid being misgendered, James might end up isolating himself from others, letting friends down when invited to social events, which ultimately would leave him feeling unseen.

In reality, misgendering is not the only source of social dysphoria, but it encompasses how we are perceived by other people. For some gender-diverse folk, the trans label is rather heavy and they fear that others would view them as 'freaks', 'sexual deviants', or simply 'mad'. This taps strongly into the last area, *internal dysphoria*. This area comprises broad feelings towards one's identity as a trans or non-binary person, but there are no frontiers or walls dividing our self-perception, and often internal dysphoria gets merged with general identity. For example, Dylan (pronouns 'they/them') struggled with social interactions from an early age and was bullied at school. Dylan developed a tendency to accommodate the needs of others, omitting their own. When speaking about their non-binary agender identity, Dylan tends to diminish the impact of being misgendered. They say they don't want to bother others by asking them to use their new name, and they repeatedly say, 'I can bear it. I always have.' But, as time passes, Dylan starts feeling increasingly disconnected from themselves and from others, and feels somewhat ashamed. In order to feel more congruent and seen, Dylan would have to overcome the childhood experiences of being put down and laughed at, as well as to find a new sense of self-worth that would allow them to assert themselves.

Considering the above, I encourage clients to map their experience of dysphoria, degrees of distress and coping strategies around each one of these. In this way, they evaluate which are likely to be resolved by gender-affirming interventions (like hormones or surgery), which by delineating new social boundaries, and which by accepting oneself and one's imperfect reality.

Table 1 Types of gender dysphoria

Types of gender dysphoria		
Body dysphoria	**Social dysphoria**	**Internal dysphoria**
What my body looks like and its gendered features (e.g., breast, voice, beard, penis, muscles, etc.)	Gender presentation (e.g., clothes, hairstyle, makeup, accessories, etc.)	Feelings of congruence or incongruence
		Sense of self, versus sense of alienation
What my body feels like and its gendered experience (e.g., period cramps, erections and ejaculation, the weight of breasts, etc.)	Language (i.e., name, adjectives, titles and pronouns)	Self-perception beyond gender (e.g., worthiness or unworthiness, belonging or disassociation)
	How I am viewed and treated by others based on their perception of my gender	
		Internalised transphobia

However, this classification of 'Types of gender dysphoria' is not yet used in diagnostic manuals, as these have only recently started to bring a more comprehensive description of gender diversity. It seems incredible to think that only 50 years ago (in 1973), homosexuality was removed from the Diagnostic and Statistical Manual of Mental Disorders (DSM) of the American Psychiatric Association, and that the World Health Organization (WHO) only removed homosexuality as a diagnostic category from the ICD-10 in 1992. The inclusion of this sexual orientation as a type of fetish promoted the depiction of gay people as deviants in need of reparative therapies. Similarly, *Gender Dysphoria DSM-5 302.85 (F64.9)* continues to exist and be classified as a mental health condition by the DSM-5 (published in 2013) and DSM-5-TR released in 2022. Inadequately, this classification fails to include non-binary identities, only considering the existence of transgender males or females. However, a revolutionary step was taken in 2019, as the WHO shifted attitudes towards *Gender Incongruence (HA60)* from being a mental health condition, to a condition related to sexual health (ICD-11, published in 2019). In short and officially, trans and non-binary people are not mentally ill but their identity is a result of natural diversity.

A brief note on sexuality

Based on heteronormativity and cisnormativity, it is not surprising that sexuality (i.e., who you like) and gender (i.e., who you are) often get confused. However, when it comes to describing their sexual and/or romantic attraction, like cisgender people, trans and non-binary folk identify in a wide array of forms. We will speak about them in detail in Chapter 7, *Sexuality, romance and identity labels*.

Models of assessment

As a gender clinician, apart from delivering therapy, I also carry out assessments to determine diagnoses of HA60 Gender Incongruence ICD-11. In the UK, these diagnoses allow clients to access hormone replacement therapy (HRT) and gender-affirming surgical interventions, either via the National Health Service (NHS), or privately. Several studies have noted that pursuing a physical and/or social role transition has the potential to significantly improve the mental health of gender-diverse individuals (Newfield et al., 2006; Olson et al., 2016).

Currently, the NHS provides funding to access most of the main interventions, like HRT, genital reconstructive surgery, chest surgery for transmasculine people assigned female at birth, limited facial hair removal for transfeminine people assigned male at birth (apart from in Wales), speech and language therapy and psychotherapy. However, there are limited resources as well as a reasonably small number of professionals who are trained to provide healthcare to gender-diverse populations. So, when it comes to accessing support through the NHS, in 2022 patients waited a minimum of three years from initial referral to be seen at a gender specialist service. There are many trans and non-binary people who live in an expectant state, as they become casualties of the delays of the system and the impact of the recent pandemic, and for this reason, those who can, often opt for private healthcare.

The wait associated with undergoing transition can place gender-diverse folk in a psychological limbo, whereby they put their lives on pause until they are able to access interventions, for example, not going on a date, or not starting that university course. As clinicians, we should more frequently ask, 'If it is not within your power to fast forward the clock to a time when you could live a fully congruent life, and if this in-between period is unmovable, then what could you make out of it?' (Scarrone Bonhomme, 2021). Some people are invested in the narrative that in order to be trans, they ought to hate the incongruent parts of themselves. This is not their own fault, but if you ask me, partly promoted by traditional assessment formats and by the limited understanding that still exists within this field. Interestingly, some of my clients tell me that they welcome dysphoria, as a sign that their gender feelings are valid and real. But suffering is not part of the criteria, incongruence is.

Gender euphoria is not yet considered as part of the assessment and is a term that refers to the experiences of congruency and satisfaction that trans and non-binary folk get from living in an affirming body or social role. For example, 'I experienced tremendous relief when I came out to work and people started calling me by my name. Even though my parents were not thrilled about me being trans, they have come to accept and understand that this is not a choice, but the result of my gender-diversity. I feel better since I am able to present in a way that is affirming to me, and even the anxiety I used to experience around going out with friends has ceased somehow.' To me, these narratives of relief and joy are as important to attend to as those of distress.

Psychotherapy and where to start

Ample research describes how gender-diverse people are more likely to experience mental health difficulties (Bouman et al., 2017; Budge et al., 2013; Dhejne et al., 2016; Rimes et al., 2019). Differently from what may be assumed, the development of these conditions is likely to be linked to the impact of social stigma, rather than anything to do with simply being trans. Counterintuitively, trans people are less likely to seek mental health support. The harmful history of reparative therapies and widespread negative attitudes towards gender-diversity perpetuate fears within these communities, particularly around being judged or exploring gender issues for the first time (Hunt, 2014). Johnson (2014) investigated the type of barriers that gender-diverse people find when accessing therapy, highlighting: the assumption of universal transgender experience, discomfort or disapproval, endorsement of gender-normative and binary culture and use of transphobic and/or incorrect gendered terminology. These experiences impacted the client's self-perception, the perception of the therapist and therapy and relationship with others. However, studies have shown that trans people find therapy to be useful and the therapeutic relationship relevant (Applegarth & Nuttall, 2016; Moye, 2018). Throughout this book, my co-authors and I aim to help you reflect upon your attitudes and approach to therapy. Let me say it clearly: there is no need to feel ashamed; we have all been indoctrinated into certain ideologies, but it is your duty to reflect on what these are and how they may shape your automatic responses.

A moment for reflection

What is said about LGBTQI+ people in your culture, religion or community? What are your concerns when working with LGBGTQI+ individuals?

The use of language

There is a worldwide movement towards the examination of our use of language, not only to analyse its purpose, but also to read between the lines, furthering our understanding of what words imply, promote and trigger in certain communities. We are becoming more aware of comments which could be construed as racist and of words which should never be used. The pretext of 'we have always done things this way' often gets in the way of change and there is no denying that it takes practice, but so do most things in life. Often when talking with colleagues about gender, I sense an underlying angst, a frozen smile that shouts, 'I hope I didn't say anything wrong and come across as transphobic.' Language has a crucial role in facilitating a nurturing and safe environment in therapy. What you say and how you say it won't escape the amygdala, so when working with gender-diverse clients, we should cautiously choose our words, but only as much as we would in any psychotherapeutic context. The truth is that you are likely to stumble at some point.

A brief note on misgendering

At the start of my clinical work with trans and non-binary people I worried about misgendering them, about experiencing the pull of someone who has a tic and is attempting to control it. Before the arrival of my first clients, I reviewed their name and pronouns and whispered them to myself. You never know who you will encounter, or at what stage of their transition they will be. Regardless of how easy or challenging it would be to identify them as they identify themselves, I questioned if my brain would play tricks on me. Luckily, this worry only materialised twice and here is what to do when this happens.

You stop, correct yourself, apologise and continue. If you feel that misgendering might have upset the client and your apology didn't suffice, then take the time to address your mistake openly, to transform it into an opportunity for reflection by saying something along the lines of, 'How was it for you when I slipped and called you by your old name?' Also, you might want to bring to supervision the question: 'What happened there for me. What pulled me to misgender my client?'

As your understanding of the experiences of trans and non-binary individuals expands, you will be better able to hold in mind how words can hurt and impact a community's public image. Realistically, it is not possible to accommodate everyone, and a term that some might find empowering (like 'queer'), to others might be triggering, transporting them to times when they were shouted it in the school playground. For this reason, always take an affirmative stance by which you address what terms are representative of the client's experience and understanding of themselves. Delve into the reasons for choosing some words and not others, enquiring about the history behind them. Through this exercise, you can support clients who might have little or no contact with their communities to understand what sort of associations other gender-diverse people might make when hearing these terms.

Sometimes it took a bit of time and mental repetition for me to be able to see the person as they saw themselves, but as I used the language that represented them, I could see a special kind of light shining through. Many might not be quite ready to be called by a different name or pronoun, or might have not even considered it to be a possibility. So, you can pose it as an option, an open invitation to test pronouns and names. Where safer to experiment with this than in therapy?!

Questions you might want to explore with trans and non-binary clients

- How would you like me to address you?
- What is your legal name?
- What pronouns make you feel seen by others?
- What words should I use to refer to your identity, your body, your relationship to your child (e.g., mother, father, parents)?

Please bear in mind that LGBTQI+ people can struggle with elements unrelated to these labels, so only focus on them if your client requests it. Some therapists might be tempted to try and find the explanation for why their clients are trans. When delivering training attendees sometimes ask, 'Is my client identifying as a trans man because of the difficult relationship with his mother?' But, as Yalom (2015) memorably said:

> the drive to explain is an epidemic in modern thought and its major carriers are contemporary therapists: every shrink I have ever seen suffers from this malady, and it is addictive and contagious. Explanation is an illusion, a mirage, a construct, a soothing lullaby.

So, responding to the question posed above, please raise your hand if you do not have a challenging relationship with either of your parents. Perhaps, we could simply accept diversity as the most plausible explanation

Table 2 Gender-affirming principles

Gender-affirming principles	
As a clinician	**Working with clients**
• Reflect on personal views and biases about gender-diverse people • Acquire trans-affirmative knowledge: existence in history, biological theories, etc. • Become an ally/accomplice • Model non-judgemental attitudes and compassion	• Support the individual's freedom and self-knowledge • Explore experiences of acceptance and rejection from oneself and others • Help clients explore the attributed meaning of their trans and general identity • Support social integration and expressions of (safe) vulnerability

On neurodiversity and gender diversity

I could not end this chapter without briefly addressing the relationship that exists between neurodiversity and gender diversity, in particular, the higher co-occurrence of autism traits in transgender and non-binary communities (Glidden et al., 2016; Heylens et al., 2018; Jones et al., 2011; Pasterski et al., 2014). *Autism spectrum conditions* (ASC) constitute a group of social communication and behavioural differences of a neuro-developmental nature that causes varying degrees of impairment – an 'impairment' that is measured against the norm and neurotypical ways. It has been estimated that approximately 1 per cent of the general population has autism (Baird et al., 2006; Brugha et al., 2011); however, within gender-diverse groups, its prevalence has been estimated to be between 6 and 26 times higher (Kaltiala-Heino et al., 2015; Pasterski et al., 2014). There is a great variability between studies, and at the London NHS Gender Identity Clinic we carried out our own research, establishing the prevalence of self-reported diagnosis of ASC in a population of 189 non-binary patients at 11.1 per cent (Evans et al., 2019).

'What is the reason?' you may ask. A number of theories have been postulated but facing such a complex issue it would be unusual to arrive at a simple and straightforward answer. In 2019, I started to explore the question, 'How do gender diverse people sense dysphoria?' After an intense and somewhat obsessional search, I stumbled upon *interoception*. Most people only ever learn about the five basic senses (i.e., smell, touch, taste, sight and hearing), however there are more. Interoception allows us to perceive our internal processes and organs (e.g., heartbeat or feelings of hunger) and, combined with exteroception and proprioception, they might hold the key to perceiving dysphoria. This is because, as previously explained, dysphoria is not only about how the body looks, but about how it feels. One of the common traits of ASC is sensory hypersensitivity, which led me to postulate that individuals with ASC may too have greater interoceptive sensitivity, making gender-diverse folk with autism traits more conscious of their internal bodily states, and perhaps especially attuned to feelings of dissonance between their [gendered] sense of self and their birth-assigned sex (Scarrone Bonhomme, 2019a). In line with this hypothesis, previous studies have connected interoception to a person's sense of self (Craig, 2010; Damasio, 2003).

Other authors, like Walsh et al. (2018), proposed that individuals with ASC are more likely to reject binary cisgender norms as they are less concerned with restrictive social norms, which facilitates disclosure of trans identities. Similarly, Kristensen and Broome (2015) focused on the challenges that individuals with autism experience when attempting to grasp the ephemeral nature of societal gender restrictions, making them more likely to look beyond traditional gender models.

Lastly, Baron-Cohen et al. (2003) provided an explanation for the higher prevalence of autism traits in individuals assigned female at birth with a transmasculine identity (Jones et al., 2011), suggesting that the *Extreme Male Brain Theory* may play a role in this association. The theory proposes that individuals with ASC have a heightened drive to systematise and diminished drive to empathise (Baron-Cohen, 2002). Studies show that autism traits are positively associated with elevated foetal testosterone levels (Auyeung et al., 2009), linked with the expression of what are often seen as traditionally masculine traits in individuals assigned female at birth. However, this last theory has been criticised for oversimplifying sex brain differences, as well as for being based on gender stereotypes that do not account for socialisation.

A nod to ADHD

Within neurodiverse presentations, Attention Deficit Hyperactivity Disorder (ADHD) and ASC are often intertwined. Among many others, ADHD can present in adults with features like lack of concentration, disorganisation, forgetfulness, difficulties in time management and a tendency to procrastinate. So, we should be aware of how gender-diverse individuals with ADHD traits can experience added challenges to transitioning, given the high degree of organisation required to research available treatments and providers, booking and attendance to specialist appointments, gathering of evidence, change of legal documents and other bureaucracy.

Understanding the challenges that being neurodiverse can pose, and adding those of being transgender and non-binary (such as the impact of minority stress), it is not surprising to find out that, when comparing the psychological wellbeing of people with autism who are cisgender against that of gender-diverse people, the latter group displayed higher levels of stress, depression and anxiety (George & Stokes, 2018).

In their own words: neurodiversity

'In their own words' is a collection of interviews of community members carried out by Skye. Here you can read their stories directly. To learn more about the process, review the Preface.

Research has shown that trans and non-binary people are more likely to report neurodiversity than cis people, and neurodiverse people are more likely to report a trans or non-binary identity than neurotypical people. While the nature of this relationship is not really understood, some have used this correlation to question the ability of neurodiverse trans people to understand and express their own gender identity. It therefore felt important to hear from a neurodiverse trans person about their own experiences. Ramona (they/them) reached out to me on Instagram after seeing my call for interviewees. They are a 32-year-old genderfluid neurodiverse person who offers peer coaching to other neurodiverse people. They responded to our interview questions in writing. Here are extracts from their answers which they have agreed to share.

The relationship between neurodiversity and gender identity

It wasn't until I learned that I was undiagnosed multiply neurodivergent that I really started confronting my gender. I'm Autistic, ADHD, Dyspraxia and Dyscalculia. I think once I started unmasking my neurodivergence, which essentially is living more authentically, not hiding who I am or what I need, I realised I couldn't ignore my gender fluidity.

A big part of being autistic for me at least is finding social rules arbitrary, which I think gender identity definitely fits in there. Even before I had the mental safety of getting rid of those intrusive thoughts, to explore my gender, I've always dressed how I wanted, cut my hair how I wanted. Being in a queer relationship, we've never had traditional gender roles of dividing chores or things like that. So, in a way I think being ND (neurodiverse), particularly autistic, means I instinctively want to be more authentic to who I am.

I have felt feminine – and loved it. I've chopped all my hair off, wore masculine clothing and loved being mistaken for a man. I've always wanted to be a drag queen and a big part of fully accepting my gender was accepting that it was ok for me to be a trans gay man. I think that was the big part that I felt like I had no right to. After letting go of that neurodivergent mask, I realised I couldn't ever be true to myself if I didn't accept this very big part of who I am.

Their work as a peer mentor

So, learning what being neurodivergent actually meant was so eye opening. It literally saved my life. So, I realised I had to help others. I don't want anyone to ever feel like they are a failure because their brain processes things differently.

Typically, I help other ND or suspected ND people organise things for self/ official diagnosis. Giving them guidance, validation, helping them let go of that internalized dialogue that tells them they're just lazy or a failure. I also help with practical things, like executive functioning challenges, tips that work for ND brains.

But really, for so many people the goal is letting go of self-hatred. Accepting yourself exactly as you are, the strengths, the weaknesses, and seeing them as completely neutral facts. I love it. It's the best job I've ever had.

Challenges and misconceptions

I think some of the biggest challenges that face trans and non-binary ND folks is a lack of empathy and understanding. It's people with no understanding or desire to understand how others could want or need something different from their life. It's thinking that their own opinions and biases are facts.

There is so much misinformation because so much about being neurodivergent is from an outsider perspective. Probably the biggest one is that we don't understand our own identities and therefore must have been groomed to think we're trans. It's just infantilising, and dehumanising.

The problem is there is no changing someone's mind who is so far gone, they are so firmly holding on to their biases and bigotry that they are unwilling to hear anything that doesn't confirm that. So, the only way I get through hate messages from TERFs or random gay men who think I'm homophobic for being a trans gay man (???) is to not give their words or thoughts any kind of platform. I won't engage with them; I won't argue or defend myself because there is nothing to argue. I'm who I am. I love who I am. I wouldn't change for anything.

Representation

Representation is so important! I know I've always been gender fluid – even if I couldn't put it into words. I remember being 7 or 8 and watching Victor Victoria *over and over because I felt something I couldn't put into words, which now I know is representation.*

That's why I do what I do, why I share my experiences as a late-diagnosed multiply ND person, as a queer and gender fluid person. As someone who is a feminine, married to another woman, and also as a trans gay man, I know I'm not alone. There are so many people out there who need to see that they aren't alone either.

2 Working with identity-based trauma

by Dr Michael Beattie

The ever-present gender police

It's a cold June morning in Harare and I am hanging around, along with around 800 other boys, on the dry grass lawn, split into rough age groups. The 1st XV rugby team are the 'gods' of my school and all pupils are required to gather in worship on the quadrangle outside the prefects' common room every Friday for 'War Cry' practice. Prefects, who seem almost like adult men from my 13-year-old vantage point, shout intimidating abuse at the younger boys, haranguing them for their apparent lack of 'school spirit' and for not chanting the school war cries loud enough in this practice for the weekend's impending game. They pick on the smallest first year boy they can find and make him stand in front of the whole school and shout the school war cry by himself. His high-pitched, unbroken voice screams out:

> *Masakati! Makadi! This is what we've come to see!*
> *Dragon fire, Dragon flame!*
> *Watch St George's play the game!*

Eight hundred boys immediately break into laughter and the little boy bursts into tears.

The message is clear. Rugby is a game played by men who exemplify masculine strength, competitiveness, violence and fearlessness. This small child, with an unbroken voice, is to be ashamed of himself for failing to meet that standard. And we are all to be aware that the same humiliating fate awaits us if we similarly fail to measure up.

Writing about this incident some 40 years later I not only still remember the ridiculous song, I can remember the look of the intimidating prefects, the slightness of the little boy and the hot flush of shame empathically experienced as he burst into tears.

Understanding IBT

So, what is IBT?

In recent years, Laura and I have given a number of seminars about the phenomenon of identity-based trauma (IBT), something that she has previously defined as:

A deep-rooted feeling of discomfort about a given identity characteristic which society has conceptualised as inadequate, problematic, or defective. Beliefs about what holding this characteristic means are then both actively and passively absorbed. These beliefs have the potential to elicit anxiety about accepting oneself or being accepted by others. This anxiety is mainly caused by the risks and disadvantages that holding that label may bring.

(Scarrone Bonhomme, 2019b)

In this chapter we explore the experience of holding an identity characteristic that is stigmatised by society; what it is like to hold that shame and stigma; and how understanding that experience as a form of trauma can unlock new ways to work with the phenomenon therapeutically.

Who is susceptible to IBT?

Anyone that holds a minority characteristic for which they may experience discrimination, shaming and alienation is susceptible to IBT. For many, IBT may be part and parcel of the experience of holding a stigmatised minority characteristic, even if that characteristic is as banal as simply having red hair and freckles. Importantly, the identity characteristic might be visible, as in the case of religious minorities or disabilities, or it may be an aspect of our identity that we can put some effort into concealing, such as our sexuality or gender identity.

We also recognise that a great deal of the stigma and shame directed at those of us with minority sexual identities has its roots in gender presentation. We can see that LGB individuals who are able to reproduce an ostensibly cisgender-heterosexual (cishet) gender presentation (in other words one that is in line with normative standards for cisgender, heterosexual people), along with other aspects of cishet culture such as normative, monogamous relationship styles, might have access to greater privilege in society than those who are less able to put on a decent performance.

But simply looking, or indeed being, cisgender and straight doesn't give us a free pass from gender-based stigma. The gay man who is 'stealth' may fear being outed just as much as the trans woman who 'passes' as cis. The terms 'stealth' or 'passing' in this context refer to LGBTQI+ people who are able to give the kind of gender performance where they are likely to be assumed to be straight and/or cisgender, and therefore blend into or can be easily accepted by the mainstream cishet community. The terms are widely agreed to be problematic since they privilege cishet ways of being in the world, something that we will explore in greater detail in Chapter 10, *What if they clock me?*. Moreover, the straight cis man who fears being categorised as 'effeminate' or 'faggy' by his friends may equally go to great lengths to force himself into an appropriately heteronormative performance, and may experience trauma in relation to being shamed. This shame may present itself later in his relationships or in the work in therapy.

Recognising intersectionality

Although this chapter looks specifically at IBT through the lens of what Iantaffi (2020) calls *gender trauma*, we acknowledge that all of us are not simply defined by one aspect of our identities, but that the many different identity categories which we hold will work dynamically with one another, affected by both time and context. Intersectionality refers to this interactivity between different social identity structures and, importantly, how interactions are productive of both relative social privilege and oppression.

Kimberley Crenshaw coined the term *intersectionality* to show how the separation of different areas of identity in public policy, for example gender identity and race, worked to render the experience of Black women invisible (Crenshaw, 1989).

As such, intersectionality is not simply another way of describing a focus on diversity and difference, it is a way of exploring how different subjectivities are productive of power and privilege, as well as oppression. Intersectionality therefore invites us to conceptualise the person as more than one prominent identity label. The experience of a young, highly educated, Asian trans man will be very different from that of a White, religious, elderly trans woman. Just because they are both trans doesn't make their lived experience necessarily similar. Moreover, although the person we are working with may have a trans or non-binary gender identity, their gender identity may or may not actually be the presenting issue and should not necessarily be the only thing that we hold in mind when thinking about their experience of the world and how it intersects with our own.

Table 3 Intersectional identity matrix

Identity characteristic	Greater power and privilege	Greater marginalisation
Sex	Male	Female and intersex
Race	White people	People of colour
Language	Western languages (esp. English)	Languages of developing countries
Class	High income	Low income
Gender identity	Cisgender	Trans & non-binary folk
Ethnicity	European	Non-European
Education	University educated	High school/trades-based
(Dis)ability	Able-bodied	Disabled
Sexuality	Straight	Gay, bisexual, asexual
Age	Middle-aged adults	Older adults & children

Look at the matrix in Table 3 and take a moment to reflect on your own intersectional identity and how it may act to afford you greater power and privilege or greater marginalisation. Is this something that you are already aware of, or are you considering this actively for the first time? How does your own experience of privilege and marginalisation affect how you feel about yourself or your ability to be heard in society?

What is trauma?

Trauma-informed practice affects many of the ways in which we think about working with distress with our clients. There are various definitions of trauma in the literature, but one rather simple and elegant definition is provided by the UK Trauma Council (2022) on their website: 'Trauma refers to the way that some distressing events are so extreme or intense that they overwhelm a person's ability to cope, resulting in lasting negative impact'.

Sanderson (2013) explores the difference between single traumatic events, such as experiencing or witnessing an accident or violent crime, and complex trauma, where a person has sustained or repeated experiences of physical, sexual or emotional abuse, or neglect within a relationship. She makes a particular distinction in respect of trauma experienced within attachment relationships in childhood where the long-term effects can be devastating. She points to how experiencing these violations from someone we want and need to be close to disrupts normal functioning of trust and dependency needs. Because of how these failures affect our sense of self, she argues that these disruptions tend to result in problems with chronic low self-esteem, a sense of emptiness and difficulties in managing trust, dependency and vulnerability in future adult relationships.

Thinking about the experiences of many of my LGBTQI+ clients, again and again I have heard similar childhood stories of verbal, physical and sexual violence from peers, and either direct or feared rejection from responsible adults who these children might have wanted to turn to for support. Even those queer youth who could pass for cis or straight experienced the trauma of witnessing the gender policing of their peers and the fear that, at any moment, they might be outed and similarly shamed or assaulted (Beattie & Evans, 2011).

The above definition also suggests that trauma is about a particular kind of grossly frightening or intense experience that has 'lasting negative impact'. The DSM-5 (American Psychiatric Association, 2013) explores how this psychological distress might show up in the consulting room and suggests that it can vary from anxiety and fear-based symptoms through to blankness, anhedonia, dysphoria and dissociation, as well as anger and aggression.

Why do we see IBT as trauma?

It is clear that many LGBTQI+ youth experience distressing events in childhood and beyond that are so intense that they overwhelm their ability to cope, including the ongoing experience or very real threat of bullying, rejection, shaming, stigmatisation and even death. Data from Galop's Hate Crime Report (2021) and Stonewall's LGBT in Britain: Hate Crime (2017a) suggests that around two-thirds (64 per cent) of LGBTQI+ people had experienced anti-LGBTQI+ violence or abuse, and that two in five trans people (41 per cent) have experienced a hate crime or incident because of their gender identity.

We know that group belonging and conforming are powerful dynamics in the creation of the self. Our safety is fundamentally predicated on them and, as Gilbert (2009) suggests, shamed or rejected individuals are less likely to survive. Gender and sexuality are particularly powerfully policed in society. LGBTQI+ kids learn that if they don't fit in, they risk being cast out and so often try to work out the version of themselves that they should be to remain part of the group. Rejection or threatened rejection from family, peers and wider society is traumatic and, sadly, often part of their lived experience. The Albert Kennedy Trust (2018) found that up to 24 per cent of young people at risk of homelessness identify as LGBT, with 77 per cent citing familial rejection and abuse after coming out as the primary cause.

We further conceptualise IBT as trauma because LGBTQI+ people tend to display the symptomatic responses of someone who has been traumatised. As we have seen, trauma is about experiences that overwhelm a person's ability to cope. Informed by Polyvagal Theory (Porges, 2011), we can see how *Flight-Fight-Freeze* responses are activated in people with IBT as they attempt to deal with rejection and shaming:

- *Flight* – for example, an escape into substance misuse and other forms of distraction, or the avoidance of anything related to gender or sexual diversity, for example steering clear of friends who are aware of the person's gender feelings and who might ask, 'How is your transition going?'
- *Fight* – as exemplified by temporary periods of hypermasculinity for some trans women, as well as the aggressive denial of one's identity and the shame it elicits.
- *Freeze* – we see this in the phenomena of disassociation, anhedonia, depressive moods and social disconnection and withdrawal.

We believe that conceptualising clients' experiences of identity-based rejection and shame as trauma can help to unlock different ways of working with and working through the issues they bring.

Growing up different

In January 2020 the writer and activist Alexander Leon (2020) sent out a tweet which rapidly went globally viral as it resonated with LGBTQI+ people around the world:

> Queer people don't grow up as ourselves, we grow up playing a version of ourselves that sacrifices authenticity to minimise humiliation & prejudice. The massive task of our adult lives is to unpick which parts of ourselves are truly us & which parts we've created to protect us.

The tweet powerfully speaks to an experience common to all people who grow up with the knowledge that something about them is disgusting and offensive to the rest of the group. The clinical psychologist Dr Alan Downs (Downs, 2005) argues in his book *The Velvet Rage* that we all start off life hardwired to want to connect with and be loved by our caregivers and adults around us, not least to ensure our ongoing survival. He suggests that, from around 4 to 6 years old, many of our parents realise that we are different and not the same as other little boys and girls and that we gradually get to understand this ourselves too. Often this realisation is given to us by our peers who notice our difference and call it out in shaming and sometimes violent bullying and taunting in the playground.

The School Report (Stonewall, 2017b) and the RaRE Research Report (PACE, 2015) contain some shocking statistics about this phenomenon in UK schools for LGBTQI+ youth, finding that 64 per cent trans and 45 per cent of LGB pupils are bullied, with 9 per cent of trans pupils subjected to death threats at school. Further, 45 per cent of those who are bullied for being LGBT never tell anyone about the bullying and less than a third of bullied LGBT pupils say that teachers intervened when they were present during the bullying. In addition, 84 per cent of young trans people have self-harmed and 48 per cent of trans young people have made at least one suicide attempt in their lives compared to 26 per cent of cisgender young people.

In a review of research on the long-term effects of bullying in childhood, Wolke and Lereya (2015) found that it leads to higher rates of depression and a tendency to internalise problems, as well as a higher prevalence of agoraphobia, generalised anxiety and panic disorder in young adulthood. Analysis of the British National Child Development Study, a 50-year prospective cohort of births in one week in 1958, found that participants who were bullied in childhood had higher rates of depression, anxiety disorders and suicidality than their peers who were not bullied (Takizawa et al., 2014). The researchers suggested that the negative effects were similar to having been placed in care as a child, and that children who are bullied (especially those bullied frequently) continue to suffer negative effects in terms of poor social, health and economic outcomes nearly four decades after exposure.

This 'growing-up-different' experience of stigma is a large part of what constitutes IBT. The trauma generally starts early-on and, as it continues, becomes sedimented in layers of shame and self-alienation. It leads directly to what Alexander Leon refers to as the work of 'unpick[ing] which parts of ourselves are truly us and which parts we've created to protect us'.

Defending against shame: IBT and disintegration

These repeated acts of violence or humiliation in relationships or from peer groups to whom we need to belong to survive create a disintegration of the self: 'I have to get rid of, split off or disown the shameful parts of me if I am to be acceptable to the group.' This rejection and shaming of the self (often referred to as internalised transphobia or internalised homophobia) has a range of effects, all of which, while painful, are an attempt to keep the individual safe and to avoid any further instances of rejection and humiliation:

- **Cognitive** – thoughts about the self that are negative and self-attacking: 'I am bad', 'I am shameful', 'There is something wrong with me'. A range of schemas and self-concepts and stories that we tell ourselves to try and make us 'better' and more acceptable.
- **Emotional** – strong feelings about the self and particularly about how we relate to others: IBT is most often characterised by intense shame and self-loathing.
- **Behavioural** – as we have seen earlier in the DSM's analysis of the psychological effects of trauma, there may be avoidant or aggressive aspects to IBT. See, for example, (Gilbert, 2010): 'I may either become submissive or attacking in response to the shame that I feel.'
- **Physical** – hunched, eyes downcast. For further exploration, see Chapter 9, *Clients' relationship with the mirror.*

Minority stress and coping mechanisms

We know from our own lived experience and from the stories that our clients share with us that attempting to live up to the expectations of rigid gender norms is stressful. Even if we find that we're reasonably good at it, there is part of us that's aware that we could lose that privilege, even if it is just through the inevitable process of ageing. One only need look to the beauty and wellness industries with their bewildering array of products designed to turn back time and ensure that we stay as close to the power and privilege of youthful beauty with its wrinkle-free, clear complexion!

So-called Masculine Gender Role Conflict (J. M. O'Neil, 1981, 2008; James M. O'Neil et al., 1986) which describes the stress men feel in trying to live up to normative ideals of masculinity has been linked to depression, anxiety, health-risk, low self-esteem and problems with intimacy (Betz & Fitzgerald, 1993). Gillespie & Eisler (1992) went on to develop a similar concept in 'female gender role stress' linked to feminine norms, finding that individuals with higher scores (like their male counterparts) were at higher risk of poor mental health outcomes including depression and anxiety (Richmond et al., 2015).

Building on these foundations, Meyer's Minority Stress Model (Meyer, 1995) explains and predicts minority stress and asserts that gay people experience chronic stress as a result of their stigmatisation. The effects of internalised homophobia have been extensively examined in the literature. It has been linked to higher risk of depression, substance abuse and suicide (Weber, 2008), restrictive emotionality and lower psychological wellbeing (Rosser et al., 2008), drug use and risky sexual behaviour (Shoptaw et al., 2009), alcohol abuse (Amadio, 2006; Hamilton & Mahalik, 2009) and overall poorer health (Hamilton & Mahalik, 2009).

Similarly, the effects of internalised transphobia have been observed in poorer physical and mental health outcomes and suicidality than in the general population (Clements-Nolle et al., 2001, 2006; Hepp et al., 2005; Nuttbrock et al., 2002; Testa et al., 2014). Bockting et al. (2020) recognised the widespread prevalence of internalised transphobia in trans clients. They noticed that many trans clients consistently experience shame about being transgender, as well as internalising society's expectations around orthodox gender performances (for men and women) to avoid the stigma associated with gender nonconformity. Moreover, they found that some trans clients actively avoided associating with other trans folk for fear that to do so would draw attention to their own gender diversity or out them as trans. They were interested in adapting Meyer's (1995) Minority Stress Model to develop a measurement tool for internalised transphobia and their Transgender Identity Survey (TIS) was found to reliably measure internalised transphobia across four dimensions of pride, passing, alienation and shame.

In my own practice, working with gay, trans and non-binary folk, I have found similar stories coming up repeatedly, with clients talking about how shame around their own identity makes it difficult to impossible for them to engage with LGBTQI+ groups or support networks, or to attend Pride or other celebrations of diversity. When they talk about it with me, they might shudder or 'get the ick' when imagining hanging out with groups of other trans folk or gay people. It's a shame-laden process that drives not only their own internal sense of disgust, but also their strong need to fit in or 'pass' as straight or cisgender.

The challenge of reconnection and reintegration

If IBT creates dissociation and disintegration of the self as the person attempts to split off, deny, reject and disavow the parts of herself that are traumatically shamed, then the therapeutic work – and indeed the life work of the individual – is all about reintegration and reconnection.

And, as Alexander Leon suggests (see earlier), all LGBTQI+ people share a common experience of 'coming out' as a way of asserting identity and starting to reclaim those bits of themselves that they previously denied and disavowed.

Moradi et al. (2009), while acknowledging the stress of stigmatisation, argue that the successful management of such social stigma can, in fact, build up resilience in sexual minority subjects. In a meta-analysis of resilience research, they found that many LGBTQI+ people had found ways to harness their experience of pervasive social stigma to drive resilience and to find new ways of being in the world that actively and positively challenge conventional norms. Testa et al. (2014) explored the phenomenon of resilience for trans people in a similar way. A total of 3,087 participants completed their survey and, in common with earlier literature (Sánchez & Vilain, 2009; Singh et al., 2011; Singh & McKleroy, 2011), they found that knowing about other trans people through greater visibility of trans identities and feeling connected through community networks and friendships helped build resilience and positivity. For all of us authors, and throughout our professional networks of colleagues working with trans and non-binary folk, we notice that supporting clients to access local groups and social support networks is key to facilitating transition and greater self-acceptance. Given the findings of Bockting et al. (2020) explored above, the work of helping clients overcome their own sense of shame and internalised transphobia takes on even greater importance and urgency.

Working effectively with IBT

Supporting clients in reconnection and reintegration

By recognising the experience of being shamed and othered for holding an LGBTQI+ identity as a form of relational trauma, we can appreciate that disintegration and disconnection, along with various problematic cognitions, emotions, behaviours and embodiments are all understandable and reasonable attempts to feel safe. The goal of our therapies and interventions, therefore, is reconnection and reintegration, bringing the person back to themselves and finding more adaptive ways of being safe.

Compassion focused therapy

Compassion focused therapy has been developed 'with and for people who have chronic and complex mental-health problems linked to shame and self-criticism' (Gilbert, 2010, p.4) and has been found to be an effective way of helping people work with defensive structures and scripts such as those that might be built by people with IBT.

Paul Gilbert noticed that clients presenting with high levels of shame and self-criticism understood the need for change at a cognitive level, but often found it hard to change their felt sense of shame and worthlessness. CFT was developed with broad roots in CBT, social and developmental psychology, mindfulness traditions and neuroscience and it offers rich and complex ways of working with shame and self-attacking schemas. However, the available space in this chapter only allows for the briefest of overviews, so we would highly recommend that you do your own further reading around the topic.

In summary, CFT comprises three main themes:

1 **Multi-mind**

   The idea that the human brain is divisible into three functional units: the *reptilian brain* that deals with the most basic functions of survival with automatic, fast, unconscious processes; the *mammalian brain* which includes the limbic system, responsible for emotional processing, learning, memory and caregiving; and the *rational brain* located in the cerebral cortex which is responsible for more complex conceptual thought, planning, imagination, self-knowledge and identity.

2 **Three-part emotional regulation system**

   Comprising the *threat system*, which pushes us away from danger and is connected with anger, fear and disgust; the *drive system*, which motivates us towards the things we need to survive and thrive and is connected with desire, drive and excitement; and the *soothing system*, which is part of our attachment/relational orientation and that allows us to experience safety, peace, inter-connection, wellbeing and contentment. CFT argues that affect regulation is connected to an imbalance in these systems and, with shame-prone individuals, an over-activated threat system and an under-active soothing system.

3 The importance of shame

We all need to connect to others' minds and feel cared for, and our orientation to threat systems is argued to calm down if we are valued and wanted rather than rejected. CFT suggests that the way we experience intimate relationships (caring/neglectful) impacts how we see ourselves in the minds of others. Shame is understood as both **external** (the social experience of being judged negatively by others) and **internal** where the individual shames themselves through internalised self-attacking judgements modelled on the original external experience. Self-criticism is understood as a process that maintains shame and, as part of the threat system, is attempting to guide the self away from the risk of **external** shame by maintaining **internal** shame. When the individual is in this state of mind, they are unable to connect with or develop their soothing system, thereby maintaining a self-concept based on devaluation, hostility and humiliation.

The CFT approach

There is not enough space here to fully unpack the CFT approach to working with self-loathing, self-attacking schema and maladaptive coping mechanisms such as we might see in internalised transphobia. Nevertheless, as with all of our work with defences, a good place to start is in facilitating self-knowledge through psychoeducation, helping the client to understand how these apparently self-sabotaging and attacking ways of being are, in fact, safety behaviours.

As understanding and the therapeutic alliance grows you might want to consider chair work, asking the client to imagine their critic:

- What is it like? Whose voice is it/does it remind them of?
- How would the critic respond to various interventions?
- What does it feel about this therapy?
- Where does it come from? When did it first show up?

Core to the work is helping the client to build their own compassionate practice, engaging with and strengthening the soothing system as a means of affect regulation and rebalancing away from a focus on threat. Mindfulness-based approaches inform much of this work with the therapist modelling and experimenting with a range of techniques that the client can then internalise, including:

- validating distress
- learning emotional tolerance and acceptance
- recognising self-criticism as understandable but unhelpful
- engaging with the breath
- understanding the role of the parasympathetic nervous system
- practising attentional control
- creating space and slowing down, even if only for a moment

- the importance of practising new skills when it's easy to do so and not trying out unfamiliar or challenging techniques when we are stressed or at a low ebb
- experimenting with visualisation, including compassionate imagery, compassionate place, compassionate colour.

Case vignette

Sara-Beth was a 27-year-old trans woman. She had come out to her friends and family in her late teens and most people, after a period of adjustment, had been supportive of her desire to transition and live in a female role. When we started our work together, she had been on hormone replacement therapy for around two years and was contemplating genital surgery. She came to see me because she was finding it hard to make a decision about whether to go ahead with the surgery.

During the course of therapy, it became clear that Sara-Beth sometimes struggled to identify and value her own needs. I noticed that most of the time she would focus on how her boyfriend felt about genital surgery and whether or not others would perceive her as 'fully female' if she didn't go ahead.

She shared many self-loathing and self-attacking schemas, constantly comparing herself to cis women and other trans women who she saw as 'more successful' than her. She saw herself as ugly and sometimes wondered what her boyfriend saw in her. She seemed to get a great deal of pleasure from meeting his needs and appeared to spend a lot of her time worrying about his feelings. She found it hard to think about or express her own needs, reporting feeling blank when we tried to explore them.

We explored the idea that she seemed to have developed a script that meeting others' needs would stop them from leaving her and that being perfect would protect her from the shaming and rejection of others. Also, she had learned to distrust and become disconnected from her own needs in the process of shutting down parts of herself and her emotional life to feel safe.

Although I worked integratively with Sara-Beth, the majority of our work was informed by CFT techniques. There was a lot of repeated psychoeducation with the aim of helping Sara-Beth to understand how she had internalised some of the norms around how men and women 'should' be – including the norm that trans women are 'not real women'. We used this psychoeducation to see how she had developed a habit of being perfectionistic about her appearance and harsh and critical towards herself, and explored the idea that the critic is part of her: a part that she built from an early age to keep herself safe.

Understanding that her harsh and self-judgemental inner critic was trying to keep her safe from the judgement of others was a 'lightbulb' moment for Sara-Beth. But understanding her processes was really only one part of the story. She could understand *why* she was the way she was from an intellectual perspective. But, from an emotional standpoint, she found it almost impossible to let go. The next phase of our work together used mindfulness-based techniques of compassionate acceptance and letting go, using imagery-focused chair work to meet with the critic to try and understand what this part of her might need.

We worked at realising how the critic getting what they needed might allow them to be a bit less harsh, giving Sara-Beth a break from time to time.

Gradually, and with greater trust built up in our own therapeutic relationship, Sara-Beth began to experiment with allowing herself to feel anxiety about the judgement of others, but to go ahead with what she wanted to do anyway, testing out whether things would be as bad as the harsh inner critic feared they would be, dialoguing with and reassuring that critic as compassionately as possible along the way.

It was a slow journey with many false starts, but a consistent, kind, curious and compassionate focus on the inner critic gradually dismantled its worst effects and allowed Sara-Beth to be able to have a more balanced experience of her own vulnerability and dependency needs and to develop some self-compassion.

Other ways of working with IBT

There is not enough space to go further into other methodologies and modalities in this short chapter, but you may want to consider working with IBT through other trauma-informed practices, including body therapies (see Kolk, 2015 and Porges, 2011)

The importance of reflexivity and self-care

Affirmative practice is built on two things: learning more about the subject area you're aiming to work in and secondly, practising reflexivity around your own experience of that phenomenon. It goes without saying that those of us wanting to work with populations for whom gender diversity is a presenting issue should work through our own material in relation to gender identity and any shame we carry regarding our own experience of gender role socialisation.

While it's inevitable that we will have our own countertransferential experiences of client material, it is vitally important that we are able to hold and contain any client shame as the result of IBT without resorting to projecting our own insecurities onto the client. On more than one occasion, both myself and other therapists who work in this field have heard client stories of therapists making off-colour quips about the *Rocky Horror Picture Show* or *Rupaul's' Drag Race* when transfeminine clients have initially brought their gender dysphoria into the room. It is clearly completely unacceptable for any practitioner to attempt to defuse their own anxiety and awkwardness about gender nonconformity by joking about it.

Moreover, making a commitment to working with trauma such as IBT on an ongoing basis is demanding for us all. We can become stressed and burned out and, for those of us with IBT of our own, we can sometimes find it hard to separate out our own experiences from those of the client. Holding healthy boundaries, practising appropriate self-care and making good use of supervision are all vital if we are to be able to continue to offer effective support and care to our clients.

In their own words: ethnicity and gender

'In their own words' is a collection of interviews with community members carried out by Skye. Here you can read their stories, unadulterated and directly from them. To learn more about the process, review the Preface.

Yan (he/him) is a 25-year-old British Chinese trans man who I met when we both worked at the Tavistock and Portman Gender Dysphoria Clinic. Aries (she/her) is a 22-year-old British Indian trans woman and my partner.

Coming out: the relationship between class, ethnicity and perceived credibility

Yan: *I think that's the benefit of being in a really middle-class or girl school is that they were already 'woke' and just accepted it and would use my pronouns .... As an east Asian person, you get stuck into this model minority theory where you are smart, and people generally think that you know what you're doing. That comes with the benefits of being believed if you're saying something with enough assurance. I don't think that a lot of my friends who were Black had that experience when they came out as trans.*

Being a trans person of colour in the UK

Uncertainty about the source of negative judgements

Aries: *Sometimes it feels like I'm being attacked from both sides. When I get a weird look from a White person, I'm like, is that because I'm Indian or is that because I'm trans? Then cis Muslim people, Indian or Pakistani people also give me a lot of weird looks. I don't know if they think I'm cis, or if they're looking at me because I'm trans or whatever, but either way, because I'm an Asian feminine person showing skin, their eyes are very drawn to me.*

Being held to different standards

Aries: *I feel like they judge me more because they feel like I should be a traditional Muslim guy and I've betrayed the culture.*

Awareness of negative judgements passing on to their families

Aries: *Having grown up in that background, I know they're making assumptions, not only about me, but about my family.*

Yan: *I can really relate to your point about wider judgement seeping back into your family as well. My mom has received a lot of questions from people being like, how did you let him do that? Why did you let him do that? Over the years she's gotten better in her response of, 'I would've rather him be happy than anything else.' And passing the judgement back onto them like, 'Why would you let your child suffer?'*

Racism and white privilege within the trans community

Generalising about the trans experience

Aries: *I've heard White trans people equating their struggles to POC (People of Colour) trans people when it's not the same, and some White trans people will feel excluded when there are spaces being made for trans people of colour.*

Assumptions that people of colour are more transphobic

Yan: *And the expectation that if you're a person of colour, your family must not be accepting as well. I've experienced some people in disbelief when one of my Black friends who was trans says, 'Actually my parents loved me, they never had a problem. They encouraged me to find who I was.' And people would be like, 'Really?' just in disbelief.*

Healthcare

Advice for White healthcare professionals

Yan: *I guess it's just not making assumptions. Letting the person in front of you lead your thoughts ... understanding that my race and my experience probably does come into it but not assuming how it comes into it.... Even including it in the conversation. It felt like something that White practitioners were too scared to bring up, like they were tiptoeing around it in case they got something wrong, when really all you need to do is let the person tell you ... as with most professions, you need to keep doing your homework and learning about other people's cultures.*

Language barriers

Yan: *My parents don't speak English very well and accessing healthcare with them as a GIDS (Gender Identity Developmental Services) patient was really hard because the translators they provided were not great in terms of translating gender stuff. There were some translations where I was like, I know enough to know that isn't right.*

Working with different bodies

Yan: *There are only two non-White surgeons in the UK for trans healthcare. I think there should definitely be more bursaries and funding* *for trans people of colour to get into healthcare, and more of a push for it. We need more clinicians that represent the whole community ... especially because skin doesn't react the same way depending on your race. You're more likely to get keloids for Southeast and South Asian skin and the care for that would need to be different to White skin. I had to go through revision because of it. So, they had to use a different kind of suture for me, but it's mostly after the fact, rather than 'let's think about this in your pre-op and how we can provide the best care first go'.*

3 Strategies to come out

Sat in a cosy coupe, I cruise the Trans Siberian route. Leaning out the window, I take in the vastness of the landscape and its greenery. It has been an enthralling couple of days since arriving in Russia, where the human landscape is made up of homogenous and stern looks. At each end of the imaginary gender spectrum, you'll see cardboard cut-out versions of hyper feminine women and hyper masculine men. In this not-so-faraway land, women's beauty is showcased as capital and men's toughness is a medal to be worn. I inspect, scan and scrutinise my surroundings, unsure of what is missing and feel an uncomfortable void pinch my stomach. Oh, that's it! No camp, no butch, no twink, not even any bears to be seen. I wonder, where are all the LGBTQI+ people? Under what masks are they hiding? In a country of such intelligence and achievement, why is diversity so punished and prosecuted?

As I write these lines, I quickly become aware of what I'll call my 'clinical privilege': the ease with which I encourage my clients to be themselves in a country with embedded rights to afford equality and to punish discrimination. Here, 5,000 km away from London, there are no streets of Soho for gender-diverse people to walk in, there are no Tuesday support groups, and only those willing to risk their safety would march at Pride in Moscow. I often forget how limiting my job would be if I were to work with gender-diverse people in any other place in the world. Hence, in this chapter, where we will focus on strategies to come out, I would like to start by delineating the political terrain that will colour your work. Although we will concentrate on what it is like to work in the UK, I would also like to ask you and myself, 'What is the role of therapy when it is not safe to come out?'

'Coming out' is a term broadly used within the LGBTQI+ communities that refers to the act of disclosing one's gender or sexual identity. Interestingly, those who fall within the norm (i.e., heterosexual and cisgender people) are excluded from making such a disclosure. You are assumed to fall within the default setting and, if you don't, you need to make yourself known. Although recently, in an intended act of solidarity, some young heterosexual people have started to come out to their parents on social media platforms like TikTok.

Individuals can come out at any point in their lives; however, many people realise their identity during adolescence or early adulthood. Among other issues, the country of residence and cultural background will mediate in this process. As a point of reference, Tuite et al. (2021) gathered a sample of 106 lesbian, gay, bisexual, trans, and queer alumni from a residential gifted school in the US. On average, students came to terms with their identity at the age of 16.6 (which is similar to that found in the general population) and they waited an average of 2.1 years to share their identity with friends, and 3.4 years to share it with family. This, of course, refers to the first coming out experience. However, for a lot of gender and sexually diverse people, coming out is a process that continues throughout their life; for example, when making new friends, starting a new job and introducing one's partner, when dating someone and disclosing one's trans identity, or when being allocated a new healthcare provider.

A reflection on revealing secrets

While working at Child and Adolescent Mental Health Services, one late and rainy afternoon I was called into the Paediatric Department where I met this young boy who drew out a heart-wrenching feeling. The boy had come to the Accident and Emergency (A&E) room accompanied by his mother. He must have been aged around 9. The reason: he had tried to hang himself. Evidently there were serious concerns as to why and I was sent to assess the situation. I entered the rather surgical room where he waited alone. He was sitting on the top of an examination bed, with his legs crossed, his hoodie on, and facing the wall. I introduced myself and asked him how he was, I noticed his shrugged shoulders and I was met with silence. I tried once more, and yet again nothing. He was tongue-tied and it was clear that we needed a change of approach. I took out my notepad and offered it to him. He seemed to like the alternative and slowly started to write his answers. Eventually, after an hour of writing about ice-cream flavours and his favourite cartoons, he started to talk. He told me how unfairly he was being treated by his mother; he was pushed and shouted at. I felt like we had opened Pandora's box as his speech became accelerated while recounting every single instance, big or small, when he had been treated unfairly by his mum or anyone else. Some of these experiences were reportable, but others seemingly harmless as described from the mind and heart of a 9-year-old. The purge suddenly stopped, and he returned to his initial position of selective mutism. I could sense his worry; he had confessed everything that was hurting him and now there was nothing but a big hole.

Secrets hold weight in our lives in ways that sometimes we fail to acknowledge. To keep a secret, you must split yourself into the knowing and unknowing parts. Also, you must classify those around you and keep an adequate level of alertness to not spill the beans. Secrets can isolate, making those who keep them more vulnerable to abuse. Messinger et al. (2021) found that, relative to cisgender people, trans people have been found to be at an increased risk of experiencing at least one form of physical or sexual violence, as well as of being exposed to multiple types of violence over their lifetime – what has been defined as *polyvictimisation*. For some, keeping their identity secret can be a protective factor and the only alternative if living in a transphobic environment, whereas for others the isolation can place them at greater risk.

So, what motivates people to come out? Coming out can be an act of liberation from one's projections and fantasies, allowing the person to uncover the oftentimes feared reality of what others would make out of this difference.

Coming out can be an act of rebellion, a refusal to comply with societal norma-tive ideals, opening a door to express one's non-conformity. Sadly, coming out is not always the person's choice and sometimes, against their own wishes and timing, LGBTQI+ people are 'outed'.

Only recently I witnessed this transgression. My client Salma, who is one of four siblings, decided to come out to her older sister Faiza, who she thought would be accepting of her identity as a trans woman. Salma's inkling was cor-rect and Faiza, although confused, did not reject her. However, Salma's parents are Muslim, and all siblings were raised in this faith. Not all of them are still active believers, but the foundation of their morality is very much tied to Islam. After coming out, Salma and Faiza were left with a bitter aftertaste, a lingering concern of what others would make of Salma's identity. This worry, and that of being dishonest, haunted Faiza. At times, coming out to one person within a larger social unit can play on dynamics of betrayal and belonging. Faiza warned Salma that she might not be able to keep this secret for much longer, and indeed, only a couple weeks later she blurted out the truth. One of their brothers had seen Salma's social media profile and was bewildered as to why she appeared so feminine. She had long hair, colourful clothing and even what appeared to be makeup. It would have been too intrusive for the brother to ask Salma and so, instead, he approached Faiza. Faiza meant no harm but was steered by loyalties within the family; she said what she knew and, in this act, she denied Salma the opportunity to narrate her own story. Salma was upset, but also somewhat relieved. A portion of that heavy burden had been taken off her shoulders. It is not uncommon for people who have been outed to experi-ence contradictory feelings. Salma was lucky; this disclosure did not lead to her being shunned or attacked, but it could have been the case.

Given that disclosing a person's trans identity can place them at risk of harm, discrimination, homelessness and violence, in the UK, General Data Protection Regulation (GDPR) and the Gender Recognition Act (2004) protect individuals from being outed by organisations. Those who have applied or been granted a Gender Recognition Certificate enjoy extra legal protection, as disclosing a person's trans identity without their consent can be considered a criminal act. For this reason, it is important that you are conscientious in your clinical prac-tice and always seek consent. Not only that, but should you refer a client to another practitioner, consider: is gender diversity part of the work they will do? Is it truly necessary for me to share this part of my client's identity and history? Believe it or not, trans people also suffer with kidney stones, headaches, back pain and a variety of symptoms and conditions where their gender identity and genital configuration will play no part. It is reflected in literature that LGBTQI+ people face various obstacles to gain access to quality healthcare (Duby et al., 2018; Sequeira et al., 2012), making them less likely to seek support when needed.

Over the years, clients have shared some infuriating stories. George had an unfortunate trip to a seafood restaurant and what he had anticipated to be an exclusive location turned out to be a straightforwardly dodgy place. After an hour's commute and with a rumbling tummy, he decided to risk his luck and honour his reservation. Unfortunately, George spent the night vomiting and, in despair, he decided to go to A&E. Seeing clear signs of dehydration, the nurse put him on a drip. She came back and forth to check on George's progress and eventually sat by his side. It wasn't a particularly private corner and yet she proceeded, 'I must confess, entering the details of your consultation today, I came across your medical records and it shows that you used to be female.' The nurse hesitated and paused, 'You are the first trans person I've met, and I was wondering if I could ask you some questions.' Sleepless and nauseous, George did not want to appear unappreciative and although he did not feel this was the place or time, he agreed. It was clear to both George and I that the nurse 'simply' wanted to be better informed about trans issues. However, she did not consider the power imbalance and how in her request she outed George to passers-by, asking him to delve into potentially painful and most certainly private experiences. I cannot say it louder or clearer: it is the clinician's responsibility to educate themselves. If querying about someone's gender history, ultimately, this must be for the benefit of the trans or non-binary person in question.

Coming out to healthcare practitioners

Therapists and GPs hold a special place of responsibility, as often they are the first point of contact for gender-diverse clients – either to seek psychological support or referral to gender specialist services. So, what should you do if your client or patient comes out to you?

First, acknowledge how important this disclosure might be to your client, and try to put yourself in their position. Ask yourself, what would it be like for me to speak about the way I feel towards my body and identity when I have no way of proving it? By this I mean, there is no MRI or blood test that could help us diagnose Gender Incongruence (HA60). Consider, what hopes and fears might I project when coming out? Now that we have raised your natural levels of empathy and have tuned them towards this scenario, I would recommend using the following questions to explore the act of coming out with your client.

When my client came out to me, I asked...

- How long have you been waiting to speak to a professional about your gender identity?
- How long have you been feeling this way?
- What name and pronouns would you like me to use?
- Who else knows about your identity?
- What sources of social support do you have?
- Are you at risk of violence, homelessness or other discrimination?
- How can I help?

In the UK, GPs can change their client's name in their medical record without a formal name change (i.e., Deed Poll). It might be that, at the moment of the consultation, you do not have enough information, but you can research LGBTQI+ support organisations and specialist services and get back to your client. It is acceptable to acknowledge one's lack of training and to ask the client to guide the practitioner on what accommodations could be made to best support them. Consider that although some people might be sure about their identity, others might not have fully realised it and they might be still exploring it. Also, not everyone who is gender-diverse opts to medically or socially transition.

What is the role of therapy when it is not safe to come out?

In 2018 I attended the 25th Symposium of the World Professional Association of Transgender Health (WPATH) in Buenos Aires, Argentina, and there I met a Chilean psychologist who very kindly shared her experience of working in the field. Pia told me about her clients having been displaced by society; there was no opportunity for them to access employment and many turned to sex work. There is great stigma associated with sex workers, and I would like to emphasise that not everybody has negative feelings towards their job, however, the lack of other opportunities for gender-diverse individuals is the issue in question. Until December 2019, the Chilean government did not recognise the existence of trans people, leaving them unprotected. Since then, the Gender Identity Law has been passed, and it is now possible for trans individuals to change their documents to their name and gender. In her psychotherapeutic work, Pia predominantly focused on drafting safe itineraries to navigate the city, helping her clients establish what times and areas they could visit to diminish risks of being assaulted. She provided a haven free from aggression and judgement and supported clients in accepting their reality. Pia worked with the trauma of previous events and linked gender-diverse people through group therapy. To me, there are two conclusions: firstly, when politics and society do not provide a conducive environment for diversity, as a therapist you can provide the acceptance that your client is denied elsewhere. As psychoanalysts might describe it, you have the opportunity to be their 'good object'. Secondly, you hold a duty to become an ally, an activist and a visible voice for those who are unable to speak.

Preparing to come out

In my experience, clients often come to therapy having partially or fully realised their identity, seeking support in building up the courage to speak to their family, friends and work about it. Just like our friend Pia (the Chilean psychologist), we can help our clients strategise. The act of coming out is infused with meaning, so do not waste the opportunity to explore it.

Questions to explore the meaning of coming out

- What does it mean to you to speak about your identity?
- What do you fear will happen when you come out? If the client discloses risk of harm to self, others or from others, please ensure that you complete a safety plan.
- What would be a satisfactory result? (E.g., to be listened to, to be understood, to be respected, to be called by my chosen name, etc.)
- What are your expectations short, mid and long term? (E.g., 'I expect an initial conflict, particularly with my father, but I hope I can provide them with enough information so that with time they can understand me. I know they will initially get my name wrong, but I would really appreciate if they try.')

Ways of coming out

Markowe (2006) said that 'coming out to family must be seen from the perspective of the individual, interpersonal, intergroup, cultural and societal viewpoint'. Considering this principle, you can support your client in deciding the best way to inform their loved ones about their identity. There is no right or wrong way of doing it. Some people write a letter or an email, and later meet with their families to discuss its content. Some set themselves up by sending a text saying, 'During lunch I would like to talk to you about something.' Some invite a friend or sibling (who is already aware of their diversity) to be present as a source of emotional support, or in the case of risk of violence, to prevent escalation or to help them escape. To frame the conversation, I find it particularly helpful to use a Mentalisation Based Model, which supports clear boundaries in interactions. The individual determines the amount of time needed, the topic of the conversation and expectations about the listening party. For example, 'I would like to speak to you for the next hour about my gender identity. I know that it might be hard, but I would like you to try and listen. You might have many questions about it, and I feel it is best if I give you a bit of time to process, so that we can meet tomorrow and discuss any questions you may have.'

One of my clients used an analogy to explain their expectations which has stuck with me. They said, 'My gender feelings are like a dish that I have been cooking at high temperature for years. It's hot and heavy, and I am about to hand it to my parents without any warning. I expect them to get burnt initially, but hopefully time will cool it down.' Whether loved ones already suspect it or not, and as this breaks their known sense of normality, many can react as if they were receiving a life-changing diagnosis. Some might struggle to hear whatever comes after 'I am trans', and this is not because they are not interested, but rather that they are trying to assimilate what this means for them and their life. For this reason, I tend to discourage clients from sharing too much information too soon, particularly around accessing gender-affirming interventions.

So, what should your client talk about? If your client's friends or family are not particularly LGBTQI+ savvy, they might not even know what is means to be transgender or non-binary. Some might confuse it with being a drag queen, enjoying cross-dressing, or even with some kind of fetish. Therefore, the first step is to explain, making an emphasis on the concept of diversity as proposed in Chapter 1, *Arriving at the world of gender*. I tend to ask my clients to provide a broad description of their experience, focusing on elements that their family might be most likely to connect with. They might split it into their sense of dysphoria (i.e., how I am struggling with the way I feel, and its impact on my life); and euphoria (i.e., the positive effect gained from realising and expressing my identity). Also, it can help to bring up plans and expectations. Some gender-diverse people feel pressured, as soon as they come out, to immediately start presenting in a gender-affirming manner or accessing treatment to make their identity recognisable and tangible to others. In other words, they feel like they need to prove themselves. To help your client avoid feeling pressured to make changes that perhaps they are not ready to make, you might want to help them to clarify what coming out means in practical teams. For example, 'I wanted to make you aware of my feelings, but I am not yet ready to present in public. However, I would like to start presenting in female role at home once a week until I build the confidence to go out.'

Coming out to your children

A few years ago, I wrote a chapter called *The age of rediscovery: what is it like to gender transition when you are 50 plus?* (Scarrone Bonhomme, 2021). What I found while researching this topic is that individuals in their midlife are more likely to have children, and often they worry about the impact that transitioning might have on the little, and not-so-little, ones. Parents wish to protect their children from change and stigma, and generally from any form of distress. It is a natural desire, but we often forget how resilient and adaptable children are. We know that parental collaboration when coming out and disclosing intentions to transition has a positive effect on the wellbeing of all parties. In particular, the parent who is not transitioning holds an important role, as their attitudes will moderate and mediate these changes, influencing the relationship between the trans parent and the child (Freedman et al., 2002; Haines et al., 2014; Hines, 2006; White & Ettner, 2004, 2007). If the relationship between parents is not to continue, it is important to help children understand that this is not the fault of the trans person, but rather that their parents' relationship, like those of many others, simply did not work out.

Indeed, it is a difficult conversation to have, and trans parents are frequently filled with fear of rejection. I have observed in my clinical practice how trans youth tend to search for acceptance from their parents, whereas trans older adults (with children) pass this expectation onto their offspring. The worry derived from coming out becomes a good motivator to continuously delay taking this step. On these occasions, it can be helpful for trans parents to reflect upon the impact that waiting has, as delaying this conversation may be negatively interpreted by the young person, as if the parent is being deceptive, or keeping a secret (Fitzgerald, 2010; Goldberg, 2010). Aside from how this conversation would change family life, we should consider that, in disclosing gender feelings, the trans parent is communicating values of authenticity, honesty, respect and trust. Implicitly saying that 'being different' from the mainstream is not a bad thing or something to be ashamed of.

Age is a factor to consider when planning the coming out conversation. The younger the child, the less likely they are to have been exposed to sufficient (and unbiased) information about gender diversity. Therefore, they might not quite understand what it means that 'Mum is trans'. For this reason, and as with adults, information should be the first step. YouTube provides a large range of LGBTQI+ educational videos and there are also books available. Parents could watch these videos with their children, demonstrating a non-judgemental attitude and encouraging them to ask questions. Challenges can also arise when parents experience internalised transphobia which prevents them from presenting the information without an implicit or explicit sense of shame. Whatever your child perceives, they might copy and feel. If the child is sufficiently young, they might go through a developmental period of egocentrism by which anything that happens is read as their responsibility. So, I would clarify that 'Mummy feeling this way' is not something caused by them. To prevent teasing at school and ensure the appropriate academic support during this period, it would be positive to communicate with relevant teaching staff about upcoming changes. Many schools organise educational sessions that help combat intolerance around LGBTQI+ issues. Setting expectations will provide them with a sense of control. Trans parents might benefit from going through a timeline with their children, delineating what are the likely next steps. For example, can I still call Mum, 'Mum', or should we start using a nickname? Can I tell my friends? What can I say if they tease me? Professional psychological support is not essential, but it might be valuable for the child to have a place separate from the family setting where they can address their feelings and set strategies to navigate the change. Also, family therapy could help smooth the process.

So, how about the teens? Goldberg (2010) found more negative reactions in adolescents, believing that these are linked to having more time and opportunity to internalise heterosexist, homophobic and transphobic ideas. However, Motmans et al. (2018) having also found this reaction in young people, believes that these predominantly relate to the innate challenges of adolescence. As I related in the above-mentioned chapter, '[p]eople change in every interaction and so, not only the individual going through adolescence or gender transition change, but those around them do so too, as they re-examine their own identity as partner or child of a person who is trans' (Scarrone Bonhomme, 2021). Similarly, Adams et al. (2004) relates the importance of parents supporting their children to explore their own sexual orientation and gender identity.

Coming out at work

The Equality Act (2010) acknowledges gender and sexual identity as protected characteristics. When coming out at work, organisations are expected to make reasonable adjustments to support their employees. Many trans and non-binary people are concerned about how their identity will be received by colleagues and/or managers. Depending on the area of work, and how accepting of diversity the field is, some trans folk might decide to change professions. For those working in larger organisations, it might be worth joining LGBTQI+ groups. Informing one's line manager tends to be the first step along with agreeing how to identify the best time to come out to colleagues. Many people opt for co-authoring an email to be sent to the team, where the tone and content will be crucial as to how the message is received. I often encourage clients to suggest that this is posed to the team as good news, whereby someone who has been struggling with their identity in silence is finally able to live authentically at work. The trans client might decide to include a brief description of their journey, or even to set some guidelines, for example, 'From tomorrow I will be going by Andrea and when talking about me you should use 'she/her' pronouns. I know this might be difficult at first, and if you get it wrong, don't panic, simply correct yourself.'

About misgendering

Calling someone by a new name and pronouns can take a little getting used to. Supporting your client to understand that people close to them will need a period of adjustment and how to make allowances is important. Encourage your client to appreciate when people in their life are using the correct name with a gesture like a wink, or later in a conversation, so that the person who is trying gets feedback on how their efforts are being met. If mistakes are made, it can be helpful to allow a second for the person to correct themselves since it might not have initially registered, and then otherwise encourage your client to correct them.

Some clients openly explain to their loved ones what it feels like to be misgendered and to be addressed correctly, providing them with a better context of the importance of getting it right. Some families might benefit from being playful, and I have frequently suggested having a 'misgendering jar'. The jar, just like those for swearing, should be located in a common area and if someone misgenders them or uses their dead name and doesn't correct themselves, they should place a coin in the jar. What to do with the money is up to each family!

If, at the early stages of coming out, calling the gender-diverse person by their chosen name and pronouns feels like an impossible task, as a stepping stone, some families might want to negotiate the use of neutral language, nicknames and pronouns. These might be less triggering for the trans person and can grant time for the family to adapt. Of course, these strategies have been devised with the idea that the person is coming out for the first time to people familiar with their birth-assigned sex and gender role and name. But how is it different to come out to someone when you have been living in your gender affirming role and transition for some time? How is it to come out while you are dating? We will explore these issues in Chapter 7 on *Sexuality, romance and identity labels.*

In their own words: therapy

'In their own words' is a collection of interviews of community members carried out by Skye. Here you can read their stories, unadulterated and directly from them. To learn more about the process, review the Preface.

I interviewed Alice (she/her) and Dylan (they/he) about their experiences of therapy. Alice is a 37-year-old trans woman and Dylan is a 40-year-old transmasculine non-binary person. Both had had therapy prior to and following transition. In our interview, they told me about some of the things that they found helpful and unhelpful in therapy. It's worth noting that many of these points are applicable to general therapeutic practice.

Unhelpful experiences

Not recognising neurodiversity

Alice: *I got diagnosed with ADHD properly in 2020. My experience with previous therapists had been before that. In hindsight, they were trying to treat ADHD as depression. I saw a really expensive CBT therapist and you can't CBT someone out of being neurodivergent. I'm angry in hindsight that none of these people seem to be trained to say you are describing ADHD symptoms.*

Pushing clients too far

Dylan: *When they would start to push me, I wasn't made aware that I could say, 'Hang on, stop. I don't wanna talk about this. I'm not ready for these things.' And so every time, every single time, it meant that I shut down and I stopped going …*

Bringing an incompatible worldview into therapy

Alice: *The type of therapy had quite a lot of spiritual assumptions in the underlying theoretical framework that I couldn't buy into. I was worried about being overly close minded, so I said I wanna give this a try. But actually, her explanations for why things are the way they* *are in the world, I just didn't believe them. She was talking about things like me picking up on stuff about my dad as a kid that I couldn't possibly have known at the time. I know you can pick stuff up from things he said or how he acted, but I don't believe that there's a spiritual force that I was gonna somehow infer something from in that way. I just couldn't get on board with that. It wasn't useful to me. I should have bailed sooner than I did.*

Helpful experiences

Letting clients set the pace and direction of therapy

Dylan: *She kept saying every session, 'If you don't want to talk about these things we don't have to.' And that just made me feel much more comfortable and receptive to the therapy that she was actually giving and the support she was giving, which was phenomenal. Since then I have had the confidence with other therapists to go, 'No, I'm not ready.' My outlook on therapy has completely changed from being something where I have to face trauma to something where I can talk about trauma if I want ... and that instantly meant that I felt much more comfortable actually talking about things.*

Being able to work with trauma

Alice: *It's quite likely that I have CPTSD from my upbringing. She is trauma informed. There was a book actually that I'd started to work through myself before I started seeing her. So we did some work through that. I haven't actually found that book super helpful, but she had that grounding there and was ready to deal with those kinds of things.*

Exploring different possibilities

Alice: *I needed someone that was happy to work through with me all the possible iterations of me going: 'But what if I'm just imagining this? Or what if I'm not, what if I'm wrong?'*

Dylan: *It might be nice to have that flexibility to discuss what gender means and where they can slot themselves if they need to, and even just discussing things like gender fluidity and expression and the differences of all these things, because gender is so complex and I was so confused.*

Letting the client direct the focus of therapy

Alice: *In our first session I told her I've seen loads of therapists in the past and I've hated them all and I don't trust my judgement as a result of* *that, and as a result of other things in my life as well. I don't feel I could be bothered to tell another therapist my life story. And with her it was, 'Let's not do that. If it's relevant, we can bring it up. But also, I know about cults and I know a lot about what it's like recovering from them. So maybe we could just take some of that as read.' And that was helpful.*

Affirming the client's experience

Alice: *Given the transphobic narratives, they make it sound as though therapists push you into being trans and actually it wasn't that at all. My therapist, despite that, did take an affirming approach and I think that is so important. If I'd been dealing with a therapist who was going, 'You're probably not trans,' I'd have been fighting them. I wouldn't have felt safe to explore why I have those doubts and understand them.*

Finding a balance between offering affirmation and information

Dylan: *I think an affirming approach is important, but if the client is coming to you and isn't sure, then it can be useful for the therapist to have that information. Not to push them into any one label, but say these are some options which might suit you.*

Alice: *The therapist was okay with me not knowing, but it was difficult for me within myself to feel like it was okay not to know. I actually would've been okay with her being more directive. Like Dylan was saying, having someone throw some identities at me and being like, 'Why don't you try this on? How does this feel?' That might also help as well. I think that's part of a therapist's job, to feel the way with the client and finding a middle ground.*

4 Arriving at the right decision

To transition, or not to transition – that is the question

Demonstrating the positive effects of having one's body match one's internal sense of self, research has shown that transitioning significantly improves the mental health of trans individuals (Baker et al., 2021; Newfield et al., 2006; Olson et al., 2016). If this is the case, then, why is it that some people do not transition? Among many others, there are social, psychological, legal and economic obstacles and individuals might actively decide to not transition or, simply, they might have no choice. Let's review some of the barriers and scenarios associated with medical and social transitions.

Trans and non-binary identities are not recognised in some countries. In others they are illegal, at times even carrying the penalty of death and, as described by Michael in Chapter 2 *Working with identity based trauma*, frequently gender-diverse folk are at increased risk of social exclusion, mental health problems, unemployment and homelessness compared to the general population (Bouman et al., 2017; Gerhardstein, 2010; Leppel, 2016; Millet et al., 2017). Therefore, when posed with the alternative between 'being myself or being safe', it is not surprising that many opt for the latter. Where legislation is concerned, many governments lack public healthcare systems, or these might not account for the needs of gender-diverse people; thus leaving trans folk in precarious economic circumstances as they try to afford transition through privately funded healthcare. But, even in countries like the UK where gender-affirming interventions are publicly funded, prospects can be dire as gender-diverse people wait for years to access treatment. It does not end there; even if they have the money and the will, it could be that, due to underlying physical health conditions, treatment is not recommended, or due to their age some might decide that it is too late. And, whatever the state of their health and their wallet, when considering the potential long-term effect of hormones and surgery, some might hesitate to embark on this journey.

In openly living as themselves, trans and non-binary folk may risk their careers, their relationships, their economic stability and even custody of their children. Consequently, when realising their identity, some might try and self-sacrifice by keeping their gender secret or limited to certain environments. In this split existence, people may find varying degrees of contentment. But whether to transition or not is not always or purely connected to extrinsic barriers; some people might not experience a sufficient degree of incongruence to motivate them to make permanent changes to their lives and bodies. For example, some non-binary, genderfluid folk present flexibly (i.e., temporarily masculinising, feminising or neutralising their presentation with the use of prosthetics) and might not want to anchor their appearance through permanent medical interventions.

Like gender itself, the decision to transition is multifaceted and, since people do not transition in isolation, some might choose to negotiate the terms and timing with partners, parents or even offspring. Ultimately, even though here I have somewhat depicted transition as a choice, we mustn't forget that being gender-diverse isn't. Time and time again, I have heard clients speak about how, in realising and accepting their identity, they arrived at a crucial psychological point (sometimes nearing suicide) where seeking congruence and transitioning was the only way forward. In fact, Bailey et al. (2014) suggested that, compared to the global average, trans people could be up to seven times more likely to attempt suicide.

Social role transition

What do we mean when we talk about transition? We could split this term into two types: *medical* which would involve accessing interventions which are permanent in nature (such as hormones or surgery) and *social*. Social role transition encompasses the steps taken towards living in an authentic social gender role, such as:

* To come out to people in one's life, including family, friends, workplace or place of study.
* To live as male, female or non-binary (in congruence with one's gender identity), using the clothes and style that match this gender and to be addressed by the name and pronouns which are affirming to one's identity.
* To change legal documents in congruence with one's gender identity, by changing one's name, gender marker or title in driving licence, passport, bank statements, payslips and even (if desired) birth certificate.

A brief note on changing legal documents in the UK

* Individuals can easily change their legal name by Deed Poll and, in contrast to some commonly held assumptions, there is no need to pay for this or to engage the services of a professional (such as a lawyer) to do so.
* Individuals can use this Deed Poll document to change their name and gender marker on official documents such as bank accounts, utility bills, university or college registration, NHS records and the DVLA.

- A person's gender marker can be changed in their passport to 'M' or 'F'. This can be requested with a letter of support from a healthcare professional confirming that the person has been living in their preferred gender role and that this is likely to be permanent.
- Regrettably, non-binary identities are not yet legally recognised by the British government, therefore, even though non-binary people can legally change their name, their gender marker remains as either male or female. However, if wishing to, they can include the title 'Mx' in their driving licence.
- Gender recognition certificates follow the Gender Recognition Act of 2004. Among other rights, it allows individuals to change their gender marker in their birth certificate to either 'M' or 'F'.

Transition timelines: what to do first

It is not uncommon for gender-diverse folk to wish to access hormone replacement therapy (HRT) prior to embarking on a social role transition. Some may hope to skip the awkward middle step of presenting in affirming clothes or asking others to address them by a certain name and pronouns while being in a body that does not quite match their identity. This is understandable but there are risks to placing all of our transition eggs in one basket. By this I mean, although HRT will hopefully aid the reduction of dysphoria and support the person in living authentically, it is no magic cure against the challenges of being a trans person in our society.

Some individuals are guided by principles like: 'If I don't *Pass* (meaning to be recognised as the gender one is, or to be read as a cisgender person), then I am not allowed to use affirming clothes or to ask others to call me by my chosen name.' In these instances, passing operates as an external locus of control, an arbitrary measure of success that couples transition to the perception of others, as opposed to the person's psychological wellbeing. I often find myself challenging these ideas, as not everyone experiences a satisfactory degree of change on HRT. This is because satisfaction is both mediated by the person's genetic predisposition to adequately respond to treatment and their expectations of what the treatment will facilitate.

For example, if Jamie believes that once on HRT nobody will ever misgender him or that testosterone therapy will make him look 'perfect' (whatever that means), he should re-evaluate these unlikely and mostly unattainable expectations. As, if these goals do not become reality, he could come to regret his transition or be perpetually dissatisfied. However, if prior to starting treatment, should Jamie start living in a male role and face scenarios where he is misgendered, he is more likely to gain strategies to navigate his reality and build resilience. Relying on himself, as well as on his HRT treatment, he can implement positive changes to his life.

Lastly, clients and clinicians must not forget that changes secondary to hormone treatment are gradual and take years to complete. Most trans and non-binary folk seeking HRT aim to live authentically, so I would wonder, why not start now? Why wait to come out and live authentically until, for example, one has sufficiently large breasts? Or a deep enough voice? However, the individual may choose to measure those characteristics. I have witnessed important benefits in those who have socially transitioned prior to accessing HRT, but I acknowledge that this order might not be best for everyone – for example, for individuals presenting in non-normative ways and for whom the likelihood of rejection or danger are greater. Hence, the person's circumstances should be carefully considered, providing tailored advice and support.

Non-permanent tools to alter one's presentation

Just like cisgender people, gender-diverse folk use a variety of tools to masculinise, feminise or neutralise their appearance. These can support an increase in gender congruency and a reduction of dysphoria. For some, these tools might be sufficiently effective in helping them manage gender feelings, perhaps to the extent of not requiring interventions which are permanent in nature. Others might temporarily use them as the second-best option while they wait for hormone therapy or surgery. Interestingly, some people report how these tools might bring further awareness of the body parts they are trying to conceal or enhance, increasing their dysphoria. A few may perceive these tools as unnatural, making them feel like they only hide the problem, rather than helping to resolve it. So, if appropriate, ask your clients what kind of tools they use

Table 4 Non-permanent tools to masculinise, feminise or neutralise

Non-permanent tools	
Masculinising or neutralising tools for people assigned female at birth (AFAB)	**Feminising or neutralising tools for people assigned male at birth (AMAB)**
• Make-up to accentuate facial hair or define jaw line and other masculine features • Shave facial hair to stimulate growth, or use of over-the-counter hair loss products to stimulate facial hair growth. Also, leave body hair to grow • Use of a binder to conceal the chest • Use of packers, stand-to-pee (STP) packers, or straps on	• Make-up to feminise facial features • Removing body and facial hair • Use of wigs and hair pieces • Covering Adam's apple with scarfs and other fabrics • Use of prosthetic breasts, or silicone breast enhancers • Tucking genitals backwards to conceal its shape • Use of prosthetic vulva • Use of padding and/or Spanx-style underwear to accentuate an hourglass shape

to reduce dysphoria and increase euphoria and what their perception is of them. In Table 4 you can see a list of commonly used tools.

The ever-evolving experience of dysphoria

Gender dysphoria presents itself in myriad ways; some people are particularly troubled by their genitals, others by their voices and some by their chests. The relationship with our bodies is ever-changing and dysphoria evolves with time and transition interventions. The discomfort caused by certain body parts can increase, decrease or dissipate. This does not mean that dysphoria is not real but that, through resolving certain issues, we might feel more congruent and less bothered about specific parts, or even hyper aware of others. For example, Emma was never all that bothered about her penis. She had lived as female for a number of years before she accessed HRT, but once she started to experience the feminising changes of the hormones, she suddenly felt more aware of her penis. A desire to change her genitals started to grow in her and, even though previously she was not particularly inclined to having surgery, after a couple of years on HRT, she decided this was best for her.

What about your body? If you are cisgender and haven't had to think about transition to resolve gender incongruence, think about your relationship with your own body and about the periods of change you underwent due to puberty, childbirth, having gained weight or even ageing. Now, consider what behavioural and cognitive strategies you might have developed to challenge the principles of what made you feel uncomfortable about yourself, and how you might have managed to become accepting of, or even content about, the way you look. Trans and non-binary folk go through the same process of changing self-perception and their relationship with areas that cause them dysphoria. For this reason, maintaining a stable sense of incongruence towards specific body parts should be used as a guidance to establish whether a physical transition is likely to be successful long term.

Medical transition

Gender-diverse people may access a variety of medical interventions allowing them to modify their bodies in ways that match their gender identity. This is achieved by masculinising, feminising or neutralising sexed features through undergoing a female or male puberty (with HRT) and/or surgery. As described in Scarrone Bonhomme (2019a), 'HRT will help materialise visual and non-visual changes to the body and while not frequently considered, other senses like smell, hearing or touch will also shift to accommodate the person's embodied sense of their gender'. Thus, as we will explore in Chapter 9, *Clients' relationship with the mirror*, these changes not only involve the way a person looks, but also how they feel. See Table 5 for a list of secondary changes associated to

Table 5   Secondary changes associated with hormone replacement therapy

Secondary changes associated with hormone replacement therapy	
Masculinising hormone therapy in people AFAB	**Feminising hormone therapy in people AMAB**
• Increased body and facial hair • Acne • Deepening of the voice • Increased muscle mass • Increased hunger • Increased sexual drive • Increased anger • Changes in smell • Hair loss • Cessation of menstruation (if this has not already happened due to menopause or health issues) • Clitoral enlargement	• Reduced body and facial hair • Softening of the skin • Breast development • Body fat redistribution • Cessation or reduction in erections • Shrinkage of genitalia • Reduction of libido • Greater connection to one's emotions and emotional lability

cross-sex hormones therapy or HRT, and for detailed information, please review Seal (2017).

Risks associated with hormone replacement therapy

We must not forget that there are health risks associated with HRT and that, in line with treatment, the risk profile for certain conditions increases or decreases to match the profile of the acquired gender. For instance, due to the effects of testosterone, the risk of developing cardiac conditions and high cholesterol increases in transmasculine people, matching the risk profile of cisgender males. Similarly, due to the effects of oestrogen, the risk of developing breast cancer increases in transfeminine people, matching the risk profile of cisgender females. Additionally, as the NHS (2020) website describes, the most common side effects of hormone therapy include: blood clots, gallstones, weight gain, acne, dyslipidaemia (abnormal levels of fat in the blood), elevated liver enzymes, polycythaemia (high concentration of red blood cells) and hair loss or balding (androgenic alopecia).

Although often overlooked, we should also take account of the psychological risks of not accessing treatments. For example, a person who experiences intense gender dysphoria is likely to present with higher levels of stress and lower mood, which in turn may affect their physical health by increasing their blood pressure or suppressing their immune system, perhaps to the same degree or even greater than if they were to access HRT. Moreover, there are additional risks to the person's life, as compared to the general population. Suicide occurs more often among gender-diverse people with lifetime rates of between 30 per cent and 81 per cent (Clements-Nolle et al., 2006; Maguen & Shipherd, 2010; Mueller et al., 2017).

Hormone replacement therapy and transfeminine sexuality

Feminising hormone therapy is likely to cause erectile dysfunction, provoking changes in the sexual experiences of transfeminine people, as well as of their partners. For individuals who have a penis, their desire and attraction may often be signalled through erections and ejaculation. And so, losing this capacity might pose challenges in terms of reformulating and understanding sexual dynamics. Interestingly, research shows that loss of erection secondary to HRT also prompts a different sort of intimacy, based not only on penetration, but on emotional connectedness (Aramburu Alegría, 2013; Davidmann, 2014; Sanger, 2010). I often meet couples who worry about the impact of erectile dysfunction. In such cases, before starting HRT, I have recommended to trial a period of exclusive non-penis-in-vagina sex to reimagine other means of obtaining pleasure, like using sensory toys, straps-on and dildos or anal play. You can find more ideas in Chapter 7, *Sexuality, romance and identity labels*.

On the other hand, some transfeminine people may wish to retain erections to have penetrative sex or to continue to experience pleasure as they have until now. This is possible through the use of medications like Viagra or management of their hormonal profile. I have particularly observed this when the person previously embodied a 'heterosexual relationship' with their female partner and where penis-in-vagina sex has been an important part (perhaps the only one) of their way of relating sexually. However, it is important to fully explore a client's feelings of dysphoria towards their genitals, erections or penetrative sex to ensure that the desire to retain erections is intrinsic, as opposed to driven by fear of losing their partner.

Hormone replacement therapy and transmasculine sexuality

Testosterone therapy can increase sexual drive in transmasculine people. Anecdotally, I recall one of my clients having been somewhat concerned during the early stages, as he was finding the increased sexual desire to be distracting. He often found himself becoming aroused, thinking about sex, masturbating and engaging a lot more with dating apps. There was nothing abnormal about it, only that it was new to him. During therapy we normalised his experience and considered how every pubertal boy goes through a period of adaptation where they develop strategies to cope with these surges in desire and arousal. But this change is also something to note and negotiate when in a relationship, as disparities in desire might arise. For example, if the trans partner suddenly wishes to have sex with a higher frequency than they did before, the other party might not feel up to it, and this might be interpreted as a sign of rejection or even dissatisfaction with their transition. But also, there are cases where increased libido is very much welcomed within the couple.

Gender-affirming surgeries

Trans and non-binary people access a variety of surgical interventions to masculinise, feminise or neutralise their bodies. As expected, these surgeries hold

Table 6 Gender-affirming surgical interventions

Gender-affirming surgical interventions	
Masculinising or neutralising surgeries in people AFAB	**Feminising or neutralising surgeries in people AMAB**
• Double mastectomy and male chest reconstruction/neutral chest • Metoidioplasty (formation of a phallus without capacity for penetration) • Phalloplasty (formation of a phallus with capacity for penetration, scrotal sac, and testes) • Facial masculinisation surgery • Hysterectomy (removal of the uterus alone, or with cervix) • Bilateral salpingo-oophorectomy (removing the fallopian tubes and the ovaries)	• Breast augmentation surgery • Vulvoplasty (formation of a cosmetic vulva without capacity for penetration) • Vaginoplasty (formation of a vulva and vagina with capacity for penetration) • Facial feminisation surgery • Feminising voice surgery • Penectomy (removal of all or part of the penis) • Bilateral orchidectomy (removal of one or both testes)

varying associated risks which can be both physical and psychological, and that will be dependent on the complexity of the intervention, as well as on the person's expectations for the surgery. As with HRT, there are risks associated with any surgery. With gender surgeries, these risks broadly encompass: risk of infection, death, aesthetics, function or sensitivity. For more information about these and other surgeries, review Ralph et al. (2017) and Bellringer (2017). In terms of outcomes, Javier et al. (2022) carried out a systematic review finding that, one-year post-surgery (or longer), most transgender patients remained satisfied with surgical outcomes.

Metoidioplasty and phalloplasty

Metoidioplasty (also known as clitoral release) involves the formation of a phallus from the clitoris. Oftentimes, the neophallus would be small, and the person is likely to struggle to use it for penetration. However, this is a simpler intervention that requires no maintenance.

Phalloplasty involves the creation of a phallus with the use of a skin graft, generally from the arm or leg. This allows for the creation of a larger phallus that can be used for penetration. It is a multiple stage, complex surgery, generally taking years to complete and requiring periodic follow-up surgeries. Many clients have mentioned how, ideally, they would like to undergo phalloplasty; however, they feel like the investment is too high, or science has not evolved sufficiently. Papadopulos et al. (2021) and Frey et al. (2016) reported that transmasculine people who underwent phalloplasty showed high satisfaction with the aesthetic result, sexual function and improvement of quality of life. However, a systematic review identified that both techniques seem to have a low success rate in achieving penetration, between 43 per cent and 51 per cent (Frey et al., 2016).

Vulvoplasty and vaginoplasty

When presented with the choice, many clients are unsure whether to opt for a *vulvoplasty* or a *vaginoplasty*. The former is a simpler intervention that involves fewer risks and no maintenance, as there isn't a vaginal cavity to be formed. Pleasure is retained as the glans penis (the most sensitive erogenous zone) becomes the clitoris, and so clitoral orgasm, as well as anal penetration, can be achieved, but doing so requires rediscovering one's body and new ways of getting there. Jiang et al. (2018) studied a sample of 486 patients, out of which 81.5 per cent had requested vaginoplasty, and the remaining vulvoplasty. Vulvoplasty seemed to be more popular among older and larger patients.

In contrast, a vaginoplasty involves the surgical creation of a neovagina that allows for penetration. To keep the cavity open, daily dilations are required. I have encountered a couple of clients for whom, very unfortunately, the intervention led to recurrent infection, making the dilations quite painful and challenging to achieve. In therapy, I provided pain management techniques, but also, we reflected upon the pressure of continuing to dilate, as giving up would mean losing vaginal depth. This, in turn, could lead to lesser sexual satisfaction, but also guilt about having wasted time and money in accessing surgery. Even, feeling like a failed woman.

Overall, satisfaction with the sexual, functional and cosmetic outcomes following either form of genital surgery has been found to be high (LeBreton et al., 2017; Schardein & Nikolavsky, 2022; Zavlin et al., 2018). Manrique et al. (2018) carried out a systematic review of 3,716 cases reporting that 70 per cent of patients were able to orgasm. Although here I am describing these surgeries in terms of sexuality and penetration, you should consider that your client might not be interested in sex, but they might purely wish to achieve bodily congruency.

In their own words: surgery

'In their own words' is a collection of interviews of community members carried out by Skye. Here you can read their stories, unadulterated and directly from them. To learn more about the process, review the Preface.

This is a combination of two separate interviews I did with trans women about their experiences of undergoing genital surgery. Josi Phene (she/her) is a 70-year-old trans woman who had undergone genital surgery almost a year ago to the day of our interview. Heather (she/her) is a 40-year-old trans woman who underwent surgery two weeks prior to our interview.

Making the decision

Josi: *I hated what was down there. The reminder, when you go to the loo of what you've got there, that would be one of the depressing things. I used to ask God to take it away and I'd wake up with the right bits in the right places.*

Heather: *Essentially the decision to have the surgery was made the moment I came out. I then spent two-and-a-half years trying to see if I could prove that wrong, and I couldn't. I've got a whole thing about trying to falsify stuff. Anything I feel about myself, especially in the last couple of years, because everything about me has been in question, I have attempted to falsify. So I genuinely did try and deal with, 'Can I be a girl with a penis?' and it just kept on coming out 'no'.*

The process

Josi: *It's a year and a day ago today I had surgery, eventually in my seventies. I went to see my GP and she listened to my story and she said, 'I'll be honest with you. I haven't got a clue, but make an appointment next week and I'll know.' No bullshit, no pretending she knew, but totally with me. Then I got a notice in May to say that my surgery date was 29th July last year. I was quietly excited. I'd anticipated it and there was a part of me that still wouldn't believe it until it was done. Something will go wrong – that was always in the back of my mind until I was taken into the operating theatre. It couldn't have gone better actually. I came home, looked after myself and I haven't had any issues but the journey was long and hard and frustrating and mentally challenging.*

Heather: *The whole process seems a bit off the way that that (the referral and consultation) works. It feels incredibly impersonal. I feel that you need to have this conversation mediated by a people person ... Questions don't really feel particularly answered. I had read all about it so I knew what these things meant, but the surgeon didn't explain very much ....*

Post-surgery

Josi: *When I came round and it was over, I suppose it was a relief, and smiling when I went to the loo the first time when they'd taken out the tubing. Do you know what? I still smile. I still catch myself smiling. Subsequently, possibly yesterday even, I had that lovely sort of feeling of things are right. I've not had a moment of regret or thought that I shouldn't have done that.*

Heather: *The basic theme of the evening after surgery was, 'Oh my God, I'm now a post-op trans girl. This is amazing. It's gone.' I was really happy that it was gone. The morning after, the surgeon comes in and they tell me that my surgery didn't go perfectly and that he punctured my bowel, which I immediately know is the worst possible complication. He described how he'd noticed it and he stitched it up. He mentioned that if it goes wrong, you're* *gonna get poo in your vagina and you're gonna have to immediately go to A&E where they'll have to do surgery. And if you survive, chances are that you will lose the 'neo' (i.e. neo-vagina). It was very scary. That cast a pall over the rest of my recovery. It then meant that every tiny thing that went wrong after that was scary .... Fortunately, I was aware that regret was likely which is good. And I think that that's really important. What everybody needs to know is that regret, particularly after complications, is really, really common .... 'I definitely had moments of 'this is gonna be the last thing I do'. 'Cause I genuinely could have died .... Having that knowledge, and expectation going in, allowed me to live with that.*

Healthcare

Josi: *The front-end reception has been some of the most awful experiences of being dealt with badly. When I had my heart surgery in hospital, I had a nurse who was a Christian fundamentalist. She was humming hymns to ward away the devil. She treated me like shit off the bottom of her shoe. Appallingly unhelpful, rude even, but I wasn't in a physical or mental state to challenge it. I had a great GP. Speaking to other trans friends, they've not been so lucky. GPs, I would say if you haven't dealt with this before, do what mine did: be honest. That is really important.*

Heather: *I was not provided any psychological support through the process. I have my own therapists who I spoke to, none of whom are specialists in it. The whole thing about understanding that regret is part of the process is stuff that I learned from my own research and discussion with friends. You should absolutely have a psychologist who meets with you beforehand, who tells you that this shit is normal and this is how this is likely to go and helps you work out a plan for managing it and who then comes in a day or so after the surgery and helps work you through those stressful moments.*

I think having people around you who understand the surgery is really important. I had a friend who'd come over who'd had the surgery a couple of years ago, the quirk there being that the moment you're a couple of years post-op you have no memory of what the first couple of weeks are like .... Some of the best help I got was from my friend who has been around multiple girls while they've had surgery and so could remember what they had been like during the days after surgery. I really would've liked to be given some sort of automatic physio going in and in the weeks after. I asked to speak to a physio and they said that the physios wouldn't see me because they weren't experts in gender surgery.

A curious note on the future of transgender healthcare

In 2017, I attended the conference of the European Professional Association for Transgender Health (EPATH) held in Belgrade. Although I was not supposed to, I could not resist sneaking into the surgical lecture on the topic of penile transplants. There I learned the reason why one of the first penile transplants (in a cisgender male patient) had failed. Interestingly, even though the intervention had the approval of the ethics panel, the funding, the professionals and the patient; they overlooked the psychological component of this surgery and its implications not only for the patient, but for his partner. The surgery seemed to have gone well, the patient was recovering and could already urinate. Two weeks after the surgery, the removal of the penis was executed as the patient's wife could not bear the thought of her husband having a 'dead man's penis' (Hu et al., 2006). In this forum, I have seen addressed the possibility of carrying out not only penile transplants for trans men, but also womb transplants for trans women, which would allow them to bear children (Jahromi et al., 2021). The future of medicine is exciting, but we must continue to reinforce the importance of our role as mental health practitioners in considering not only what is possible, but what are the implications to the patient's psychological wellbeing.

Challenging normativity

In comparison to cisgender people, there is little representation of trans folk in advertisements, movies or the media, making us mostly exposed to cisgender bodies, which then become the benchmark for normativity. This means that, for some cis and trans people, the idea of non-cisnormative body configurations might seem foreign, leading them to question the veracity of a person's gender and dysphoria (e.g., how can you be a man if you do not have a penis?). Many gender-diverse folk (particularly non-binary people) are content and even happy with having non-normative body configurations. However, sometimes, gender-diverse folk might feel pressured in aiming to attain a 'normal body'. This pressure does not only come from society, but in many countries there are still legal frameworks forcing trans people to undergo interventions which they might consider to be unnecessary. As an example, reported by TGEU (2022), the Czech government continues to force the sterilisation of trans people who desire to obtain legal gender recognition. This is to say, if you want to have your name and gender match your identity, you must have genital surgery.

It is undeniable that the boundaries between society and people are porous, and we might all be inadvertently influenced by normativity ideals. So, it might be appropriate to explore with your clients: are they electing to have certain interventions to achieve congruency? Are they strongly guided by society's standards or normalcy, beauty or even legality?

Fertility

The accessibility of information around gender diversity means that more people are realising their gender earlier in life. I commonly work with 18-year-olds
who, after years of waiting, are ready and very much looking forward to transition. Even though as standard practice I address fertility preservation, I have
found that not many opt to explore this option. Public funding and affordability,
a lack of a desire to have biological children and, especially, an added waiting
period to access hormone therapy become the reasons to say, 'Thanks, but I
will pass.' Sometimes I wonder if any of them will come to regret it, as, during
early adulthood, not many are yet attuned to a desire to be parents. Ultimately,
our role as practitioners is to provide sufficient information so that the person
can make an informed decision. In this case, note that the UK government
provides funding for fertility preservation, though in practice, access to this
service through the NHS is currently contingent on local Clinical Commission-
ing Group decisions on fertility service funding for all patients in that area, not
just trans patients.

On the other hand, individuals who access fertility preservation might
require emotional support. As we have seen, transfeminine people often experience dysphoria towards their genitals, erections and ejaculation. The process
of entering a fertility clinic to provide a sample can be anxiety provoking for
anyone, but trans people might additionally experience dysphoria. In the case
of individuals AFAB wishing to freeze their eggs, they are provided with a hormonal regime to increase the production and quality of eggs. Some describe
dysphoria towards the knowledge of having 'female hormones' in their system,
but also emotional swings and anxiety towards the process of extraction.

What if I regret it?

Trans lives have been sensationalised by the media, and when things don't go
as planned there are a lot of people waiting to say, 'I told you so.' A lot could be
said about detransition, but a key differentiation we must make is that not
everybody who detransitions regrets the journey they have been on. Danker
et al. (2018) studied a sample of 22,725 people, reporting a regret rate of 0.3 per
cent, which is much lower than one might expect from the frequency this issue
is publicly mentioned. Additionally, Wiepjes et al. (2018) identified a decline in
the rates of regret, which has been linked to an improvement in surgical outcomes (Defreyne et al., 2017; Dhejne et al., 2014; Lawrence, 2003). Also, Skye
and colleagues carried out a study looking at the prevalence of detransition,
finding that, out of a sample of 3,398 trans and non-binary people attending the
NHS Adult Gender Identity Clinic formerly based at Charing Cross Hospital,
0.47 per cent of the sample expressed transition-related regret or detransitioned (Davies et al., 2019). Personally, out of about 500 trans and non-binary
clients I have worked with, two people were seeking support due to their decision to detransition, and so my input can only be limited in this issue, perhaps
testifying to its infrequency. What I learned from these clients is that feelings
of shame and isolation are common for individuals who seek to detransition,

having lost the support of trans groups and worrying that their experience might further stigmatise trans communities. Also, they might continue to experience body dissatisfaction due to retaining features of the gender they embodied or struggling to access reconstructive surgery. Overall, I would advise to be particularly compassionate with these clients as they might be at increased psychological risk.

In their own words: detransition

'In their own words' is a collection of interviews of community members carried out by Skye. Here you can read their stories, unadulterated and directly from them. To learn more about the process, review the Preface.

Detransition is currently a very controversial topic. While research shows that rates of detransition are very low, individual cases have been used to argue for greater restrictions to transition, or that people should not transition at all. Detransition is overwhelmingly spoken about in negative terms, as a 'failed transition'. From conducting our own research into detransition, we know that the topic is much more nuanced than that. We therefore wanted to speak with someone who had actually been through the process and could talk about what it was like. Here are extracts from my interview with Ky (she/her), a transmasculine genderqueer butch, about her experiences of detransition.

Ky's experience

Motivations to detransition

When I was in my mid-twenties I realised I hadn't lived as an adult butch woman and I kind of felt like that was always part of who I was and I felt that that part hadn't been seen ....

I had some doubts over the course of my transition. It had been easier to be read as a trans guy. When I was read as a butch woman or people couldn't tell what sex or gender I was, people would get a lot more hostile and I got a lot of harassment and abuse. So I wondered, 'Did I transition to just blend in?' I had these questions like, 'Could this be internalised misogyny?' I don't think it was wrong to explore that. The problem was that I got involved with these people who said this is definitely what's going on, without giving me space to really figure out if it really was or not.

Being drawn in to Trans Exclusionary Radical Feminist (TERF) spaces

There weren't a lot of resources. I'd been living as a man for most of my adult life. How do I go from that to living as a butch woman? What does that look like? I had no idea .... So I was exploring living as a butch woman when I fell in with the TERFs because they love the story of 'trans men are just confused lesbians'....

They tried to give me answers and in some ways that was very compelling, because I was uncertain and freaking out. Having a group to tell me what to do with rules to follow with an explanation, that was really appealing.

Leaving TERF spaces

I thought the ultimate problem was the patriarchal society so it didn't really make sense for people to ally with these patriarchal Christians and then go after trans people unless they just hated trans people. Then I couldn't really deny that. Also, there was a bunch of different things like I was suppressing myself and it got harder to suppress my gender queerness and transmasculinity.

Supporting people who detransition

The need for spaces to discuss detransition

Connecting with people online can be really helpful, but I also know how important it can be to actually meet people in real life. Unfortunately, the only in-person groups that I know of that have done that are the transphobic ones.

Expectations and fear of failure

I feel like there's this expectation put on trans people who transition that it has to work out and, if it doesn't work out, then everything the transphobes say about us is true. Let's take that away and treat us like people. Sometimes life is unexpected or sometimes something goes wrong but you can put stuff in place to help people detransitioning or retransitioning.

What's good for 'detrans' people is also good for trans people

You can't really separate what detransitioned people need and what trans people need in general. A lot of it ends up being the same. Services for detransitioned people could be integrated into already existing stuff for trans people.

Representation

There needs to be more stories of people who detransition just living their lives. I feel it's always turned into these very dramatic or sensational or controversial things. A lot of my life as a detransition person was pretty unremarkable. I still had a job, had to deal with many of the same problems other people do. People who detransition are just people who have a lot of the same needs that a lot of trans people do. The way stuff gets sensationalised or politicised doesn't help. It doesn't have so much power, if you just put it out there and look at it in the light.

Reconsidering the aims of detransition research

It would be good if there was more research focused on what detransitioning people need and what's gonna help them. There's not enough of that. A lot of times people who detransition are seen more as evidence than people. That was something I dealt with a lot. People were more interested in how my experiences could be used to prove or disprove this or that idea or argument than being like – what do you actually need?

Advice to therapists

Allowing open exploration

A good therapist would try to give people spaces to ask questions and explore without any preconceived outcome or without trying to pressure people. People really need just space where their self-knowledge and needs are centred and not trying to push people in either a pro-trans or anti-trans direction. People need to stop trying to project on people who detransition or get wrapped up in their own insecurities or anxiety, and just give people space.

Getting comfortable with detransition

I've heard from some detransition folks that sometimes they felt the therapists are trying to put a certain narrative on them. You don't necessarily have to remind someone that they can always identify as non-binary. On one hand you have people who wanna use detransitioned people's stories to invalidate all trans people. But on the other hand, you have people who are uncomfortable with the idea of how detransition can call transness into question. So they're like, 'Oh, are you sure? You're not just some kind of trans?' It's: 'We want you to identify this way because it'll make us feel more comfortable.'

5 | Beyond the gender binary

By Skye Davies

About me

It is important that any piece of work about a specific community involves its members, particularly if they are a marginalised group. I am grateful to have been invited to write this chapter and to have the opportunity to share my knowledge and perspective as a non-binary trans person. I would also want to stress that I am one individual speaking from a particular position and my experience should not be taken to be representative of trans communities as a whole.

Introduction: the perfect interruption

It's a warm afternoon in June and I'm sitting in a café in Shoreditch writing out my notes for this chapter. I've spent the minimum amount of money I felt would be socially acceptable to justify a three-hour writing stint there (£2.60 on a strawberry smoothie). With *OK Computer* playing through my headphones, it takes me a while to realise that the woman sitting at the table next to me has been trying to get my attention. Once I notice her, I take off my headphones and lean over.

'Hi, I'm sorry to bother you, I was just wondering. Are you a writer?' she asked. I felt flattered by the question and responded slightly bashfully.

'Oh … not really. Well … sort of … I'm about to be ….' (Impromptu conversations are not my strong point.) I then proceeded to tell her about the chapter and the book. She paused for a moment and then delivered the line that so many trans and non-binary people are used to hearing from strangers:

'Do you mind if I ask you a personal question?'
I braced myself. 'Go for it'.
'What gender are you? I can't figure out … which way round you are.'

I couldn't help but laugh. I'd never heard it phrased quite that way before. I then had to make the decision of whether and how much I disclose to this stranger about my gender. Do I give a quick and dirty, pseudo-binary version to save time? Or do I go into the details of the gender binary and non-binary identity? (The ol' Gender 101.) I decided on the latter. My explanation was followed with further questions. She asked about my transition, my body, my sex life and libido, some of which I answered and others I politely skirted before turning back to my work.

Despite the intrusion, I couldn't help but smile. I now had a perfect anecdote to open the chapter with and one which encapsulates several elements of the non-binary (and wider trans) experience, namely: a confusion and curiosity from others towards our bodies; a well-meaning desire to learn paired with intrusive questions; having to decide whether we explain our genders to others and, if we do, how much of that we disclose; the challenge of maintaining boundaries around a topic which is private; and the retrospective worry of whether I had been a Good Trans Person™ and explained things clearly enough.

For many people, non-binary identities may feel new or unfamiliar and feeling curiosity about our genders is understandable. Unfortunately, many non-binary people find themselves in situations where they are either expected to explain, or even justify, their identities to others, or keep them hidden altogether. This point is particularly important in therapeutic settings. When trans and non-binary clients come seeking medical or therapeutic support, their time should not be taken up satiating the curiosity of those who are there to support them. It is important that those of us who are in helping professions do our own research about the populations we are working with so that we do not burden our clients with intrusive questions. I hope that this chapter can be a part of that learning process.

What is non-binary?

Non-binary people are those who do not identify as either exclusively male or female. 'Non-binary' can be used both as an identity in and of itself, as well as an umbrella term which covers a number of other identities, all of which sit outside of the binary system of gender. As with binary trans people, non-binary people may undergo social and physical changes (e.g. HRT, surgeries, name and pronoun change, voice therapy) to manage gender dysphoria, achieve gender euphoria and express their gender identity to others.

There are myriad ways in which the gender identities of non-binary people are experienced and expressed. This is reflected by the diversity of terms used by non-binary people to describe themselves, some of which are listed in the box on Common non-binary gender identities.

These are commonly used definitions, but the way that these terms are understood and applied will vary from person to person. Different gender identities are not necessarily mutually exclusive, and some people may hold multiple gender identities which resonate with them in different ways.

Common non-binary gender identities

- *Genderqueer*, similarly to non-binary, is often used to describe a gender identity which is neither exclusively male nor female. For some, it may also have political connotations of deliberately queering ideas around gender.
- *Genderfluid* is used by people whose sense of gender identity may change across time or context. A genderfluid person may feel more masculine on one occasion, or in a particular setting, and feel more feminine in others.

- *Agender* is used to denote a lack, or a rejection, of gender identity.
- *Bigender* is used by people with more than one gender identity which may be experienced simultaneously or alternatingly.
- *Transfeminine* is used by trans people who identify as feminine (this term may refer to both non-binary transfeminine people and trans women).
- *Transmasculine* is used by trans people who identify as masculine (this term may refer to both non-binary transmasculine people and trans men).
- *Demigirl* is used by those who partially identify as a woman or girl.
- *Demiboy* is used by those who partially identify as a man or boy.
- *Neutrois* is used to denote a gender-neutral identity.
- *Androgyne* is used to denote a gender identity which may be a blend of male and female, or masculine and feminine.

'Trans and non-binary': a matter of classification

The phrase 'trans and non-binary' is often used to refer to anyone who does not identify with the sex assigned to them at birth, however it does not refer to two discrete categories. In the 2015 US Transgender Survey (N = 27,715), 35 per cent of respondents reported having a non-binary identity, with the other 65 per cent reporting binary trans identities (James et al., 2016). Of the non-binary respondents, 82 per cent said that they were also comfortable with the term 'transgender'.

A systematic review in 2019 found that, while there are differences in the health needs of non-binary and binary trans people, only 11 studies had explored this difference (Scandurra et al., 2019). It seems that the overlap between trans and non-binary identities can result in the particular experiences of non-binary people being subsumed into those of binary trans people.

In addition, the idea of a clear distinction between binary trans and non-binary people is challenged by the fluidity and varying degree to which people hold a non-binary identity (Barker & Iantaffi, 2017). Some people may identify with particular non-binary labels, some may not identify with labels but having a general feeling of not being male or female and some may straddle the divide and identify as 'non-binary women' or 'non-binary men'. The idea of a strict binary/non-binary binary also risks framing the healthcare needs and treatment pathways of non-binary people as fundamentally different from those of binary trans people (Vincent, 2019).

Evolving language

As our understanding of gender develops, so too will the language that describes it. It is important that we remain open to learning new concepts and terms as they arise. A more comprehensive and regularly updated list of non-binary identities, pronouns and terminology can be found at (*Non-binary.Wiki*, n.d.)

Pronouns

In English, pronouns which refer to a person are usually gendered, 'she/her/hers' for a woman and 'he/him/his' for a man. Many non-binary people use gender neutral pronouns to convey their gender identity, the most commonly used is the singular third person pronoun: 'they/them/their'. Non-binary people may also use the feminine and masculine gendered pronouns, neopronouns (e.g., ze/hir, fae/faer), and some use 'it/its'. The pronoun 'it' has often been used to dehumanise members of marginalised groups, including trans people. It is therefore important to only use this pronoun for people who have specifically requested it. Some non-binary people use a combination of different pronouns to represent different aspects of their gender identity. If you're not sure of someone's pronoun, a safe bet is to use 'they/them' until you can check. It is completely acceptable, and good practice, to ask someone what pronouns they use.

Using non-binary people's pronouns

- Referring to Skye (she/they): 'Did you see Skye's latest Instagram post? She really needs to tidy her room. If only they weren't so busy writing that book chapter...'
- Referring to Rain (he/they/it): 'Did you see Rain after its top surgery? It looks so much happier with itself!' 'Rain said he can't come out this weekend. It had a long week. I hope they get some rest!'
- Referring to Aendra (ze/hir): 'Aendra uses neopronouns. Ze likes how neopronouns express hir non-binary identity more explicitly than traditional pronouns.'

For some people, it may initially feel strange to refer to an individual using 'they/them/their' because they believe that these pronouns are only used when referring to multiple people. However, we use the singular 'they' all the time when referring to an individual whose gender is unknown. For example, 'Oh look, someone left **their** copy of *A Game of Thrones* here. I hope **they** come back to collect it.' In fact, the singular 'they' has been used in the English language since the fourteenth century (Baron, 2018). Although this is interesting from a linguistic and historical point of view, using someone's correct pronouns is not something which requires justification.

If you do misgender someone, the best thing to do is to correct yourself and move on with the conversation. Becoming overly apologetic and self-flagellatory can end up centring your own feelings of guilt and may put pressure on the trans person to reassure you that 'it's okay' when it might not be. On the other hand, getting upset at being corrected may make the trans person feel that they can't correct you in future and cannot have their correct pronouns used without upsetting you.

Trans people can usually pick up on the difference between a genuine mistake and intentional misgendering. However, consistent misgendering, whether accidental or not, can be distressing and trigger feelings of dysphoria or anxiety. It can also have a negative impact on our sense of safety and trust, and our ability to be emotionally vulnerable with somebody. This in turn can have a serious impact on the quality of the therapeutic relationship with a trans or non-binary client. If you do find yourself struggling to get someone's pronouns correct, I recommend practising using their pronouns in a sentence out loud either on your own or with somebody else (not the person whose pronouns you're learning). Using the correct language to refer to someone's gender (including their name, pronouns and gender identity) is a simple but important way of showing respect for someone, affirming their sense of self and enabling them to feel safe (The Trevor Project, 2022).

Abbreviations

You may see 'NB' used as an abbreviation for non-binary. However, many Black activists have requested that this abbreviation not be used to refer to non-binary people as it is already used to refer to non-Black people. Some non-binary people use 'enby' to mean non-binary (a pronunciation of the initials 'NB').

Deadnames

If you are aware of a trans person's deadname, that is, the name given to them at birth which they no longer use, do not use it in any situation unless absolutely necessary, or unless the trans person has explicitly said that they are comfortable with this.

The gender binary in its historical context

Historically, the English language has not had the terminology to describe the full breadth of gender experiences and therefore many of the terms used by non-binary people have emerged in the last few decades. However, the recent development of such language should not be taken to mean that gender diversity is a recent phenomenon. Many cultures throughout history and around the world today have gender systems with more than two genders.

The *Hijra* or *Kinnar* have been part of the culture of South Asian countries such as India, Pakistan and Bangladesh since antiquity. They are people who are assigned male at birth, who identify with and express femininity. Historically, they have held spiritual and ceremonial roles as performers. In 2014, they were legally recognised by the Supreme Court of India as 'third gender'. 'Two-spirit' is an umbrella term coined in 1990 and used by many Native American people to refer to gender identities which are neither male nor female. There are over 100 Native American tribes that have more than two genders. Their specific names and roles vary between tribes. For example, in Diné culture, the *Nadleehi* are people who were assigned male at birth who embody femininity or express gender fluidity. They may hold important social and ceremonial roles. *Muxes* have been part of Zapotec culture in Oaxaca since pre-colonial times. They are people who are assigned male at birth and express femininity. They may take on social roles and wear clothes associated with either men or women. Many *Muxes* describe themselves as 'Mexico's third gender'. Since 1976, they have celebrated the annual festival of *La Vela de las Auténticas Intrépidas Buscadoras del Peligro*, which can be translated to The Vigil of the Authentic Intrepid Danger Seekers.

When considering the diversity of gender across cultures, it is important that we recognise the specific meanings and roles associated with these identities, rather than conflating them together into a single, homogenous 'third gender' (Towle & Morgan, 2006). We should also be careful not to apply language to cultures that do not themselves use that language. Many culturally-specific gender identities would not be considered 'non-binary' as the cultures they come from do not have a binary gender system to contrast against. They may not use the terms 'trans' or 'transgender' either. It is also important that these identities are not appropriated by people outside of these cultures. For example, many Native American people have expressed concern over the use of the 'two-spirit' identity by non-Native people in North America who do not understand its cultural significance (Minosh, 2016).

The array of different gender systems is extensive and beyond the scope of this section to fully explore. However, our awareness of this gender diversity is limited because of the suppression of these identities and traditions through European colonialism.

> In truth, it's not gender variation that's a recent invention, but the Western binary that abnormalizes it … gender expressions outside of a rigid male/ female dichotomy are as old as civilization. The reason it seems contemporary is due to its ferocious eradication from history and common knowledge.
>
> Marshall, 2020

When European settlers encountered cultures with multi-gender systems, they brought with them a rigid and binary understanding of gender and sexuality which was imposed onto indigenous peoples through violence (binaohan, 2014). This intolerance also had a religious element, with the Christian colonisers judging behaviours which transgressed the gender binary and heteronormativity to be sinful (Flores, 2020). This condemnation and erasure of gender identities and same-sex attraction was eventually codified through heteronormative and cisnormative legislation, which has had a lasting impact on these communities (Marshall, 2020). For example, in 1871, authorities of the British Empire passed the Criminal Tribes Act in India which labelled the country's *hijra* community, who were considered to transgress the gender binary, a 'criminal tribe'

(Hinchy, 2019). This led to widespread discrimination and violence against the *hijra* community which, despite their recent legal recognition, continues to today (Loh, 2014).

A global historical perspective shows us that the gender binary as many of us know it is not a universal law, but rather a construct which has been exported around the world and imposed onto other cultures through colonialism. It demonstrates that the dominant narratives that we are taught are told from cisnormative, heteronormative and White perspectives which have sought to erase identities that challenge their hegemony.

Clarifying a few myths

I've encountered several misconceptions about non-binary people through personal experiences and conversations with other non-binary people, as well as in professional settings. These misconceptions seem to be rooted in a mindset which privileges, and takes more seriously, binary identities over non-binary ones. I've even encountered this mindset in non-binary people who have internalised these misconceptions and see their gender identities as being less 'valid' than those of binary trans people. It is important that we are aware of these ideas so that we can recognise and challenge them not only in the clients we work with, but also in ourselves.

Non-binary people are less 'certain' about their gender than binary trans people

Uncertainty and doubt are something we all experience. It's part of the human condition. It's only natural that non-binary people will have moments of uncertainty about their gender, as will binary trans people, as will some cis people. There is no evidence to suggest that non-binary people experience any more uncertainty than others about their gender. What is important for therapy is being able to hold space for clients to explore their uncertainty and doubts in a way which feels safe and contained.

Non-binary identity as a stepping stone towards a binary trans identity

I once had a trans woman ask me, after I told her I was non-binary: 'Oh, any reason you're not transitioning fully?' Some people see non-binary identity as a half-way point between a cisgender and binary trans identity. This is a linear and soft binary way of understanding gender and transition. It is true that some binary trans people identify as non-binary for a period while exploring their gender identity. It is also true that, for some people, a binary trans identity is the 'stepping stone'. Some who initially identified as binary trans later come to realise that they are in fact non-binary. This may be because of a shift in their sense of gender, or their gender identity was always non-binary but they didn't have the language to understand or express it. Non-binary is not Trans Lite. It is an identity in its own right and what it means to 'fully transition' will be different for each person.

Non-binary identity is 'the third gender', characterised by androgyny or gender neutrality

A common frustration I've heard from non-binary people is the framing of non-binary identity as a third gender category in and of itself, with its own specific associations (e.g. we all present androgynously and use exclusively gender-neutral language). Basically, replacing the gender binary with a gender *trinary* (I was hoping that I had coined a new term but I Googled it and many, many people had already thought of this). While some non-binary people identify as androgynous and express themselves in a way which may be considered 'gender neutral', others do not. Non-binary identity and expression can involve playing with gendered concepts and language, embracing fluidity, leaning into masculinity, femininity or pure gender fuckery.

People identify as non-binary because it's 'fashionable'

Awareness of non-binary people has certainly increased over recent years. A survey by the Pew Research Centre found that the number of people who know someone who uses gender-neutral pronouns has increased from 18 per cent in 2018 to 26 per cent in 2021 (Minkin & Brown, 2021). While the historical absence of non-binary options in research and censuses makes it hard to gauge exact demographic changes over time, there certainly seems to have been an increase in the number of people *openly* identifying as non-binary over the past decade or so.

Some have taken this to mean that identifying as non-binary has become 'fashionable' and is spread through a process of 'social contagion' (note the pathologising language). This hypothesis, dubbed 'rapid onset gender dysphoria' has been used as a basis to dismiss non-binary gender identity, particularly for young people. It has been refuted by research which has found no link between the onset of gender dysphoria and increased support from peers (Bauer et al., 2022). The more likely explanation is that over recent years there has been an increase in the visibility, understanding and acceptance of trans and non-binary identity which has allowed more people to explore and express their gender identity in a way they didn't feel able to previously.

Non-binary people do not experience gender dysphoria or euphoria

Many non-binary people experience gender dysphoria and euphoria, and undergo social and physical transitions in order to address these feelings. Euphoria for non-binary people may come from being read as either masculine or feminine, or neither, or both. For some, euphoria comes when others cannot tell what their gender is.

Conflation of non-binary identity with intersex conditions or diversity of sexual development (DSD)

I have heard a few people make the assumption that being non-binary is the same as being intersex or DSD. People with intersex conditions or DSD have variations in their physical sex characteristics (e.g. chromosomes, genitals, hormones) which fall outside of expected ranges for the male–female sex binary. Non-binary, on the other hand, refers to a person's sense of gender identity and does not tell you anything about their body. Some non-binary people are also intersex, but these are separate things.

Working with non-binary identity

Mental health

Little research has been done on the particular mental health needs of non-binary people (Matsuno & Budge, 2017). Historically, studies of trans mental health have either not included non-binary people or failed to differentiate them from binary trans people. What research is available offers mixed results.

In the 2015 US Trans Survey, 49 per cent of non-binary respondents reported serious psychological distress, compared with 35 per cent of binary trans people (James et al., 2016). A 2019 review of the research on non-binary health found studies reporting more positive life satisfaction and fewer health-related risk behaviours for non-binary people compared with binary trans people (Scandurra et al., 2019). The same review identified other studies which found that poorer mental health outcomes, greater substance use and lower self-esteem for non-binary people compared with binary trans people. A study by de Graaf et al. (2021) found that a stronger identification with a non-binary identity was associated with experiencing more psychological difficulties.

This research indicates a difference in the mental health experiences of non-binary and binary trans people. This may stem from the particular experience of having a non-binary identity while having to navigate a society constructed around a gender binary (Barker & Iantaffi, 2017). Many non-binary people have described, in one way or another, a feeling of *binary fatigue*: a sense of exhaustion from navigating a society into which we do not neatly fit. Two common topics which arise when supporting non-binary people are identity erasure and exploration.

Non-binary erasure

Non-binary erasure can occur on many levels including: the lack of non-binary representation in media, day-to-day misgendering, the pervasive use of binary language (e.g., 'ladies and gentlemen'), the outright denial of the existence of non-binary identity, systems from dating apps to healthcare records which give only binary options, and the lack of legal recognition for non-binary people in the UK. Many countries have legally recognised non-binary or 'third' genders, including Argentina, Australia, Austria, Canada, Colombia, Denmark, Germany, Iceland, India, Ireland, Malta, Nepal, the Netherlands, New Zealand and Pakistan. In the UK, however, non-binary people are unable to have our correct gender identities reflected on legal documents, such as birth certificates, passports and death certificates.

Non-binary erasure has also permeated the field of trans healthcare. Until recently, the diagnostic criteria for accessing gender-related healthcare did not acknowledge the existence of non-binary people and described gender in exclusively binary terms. Until 2013, the official diagnosis listed in the Diagnostic and Statistical Manual of Mental Disorders by the American Psychiatric Association was *Gender Identity Disorder* which denotes '[a] strong and persistent cross-gender identification' with frequent reference to 'the other sex' (American Psychiatric Association, 2000). Until 2019, the official diagnosis listed in the International Classification of Diseases used by the World Health Organization was *Transsexualism* which described '[t]he urge to belong to the opposite sex ...' (World Health Organization, 1992).

Both organisations have subsequently updated their diagnostic criteria to include non-binary people. However, the historical binary framing of gender in the field of trans healthcare has resulted in many non-binary and binary trans people being denied access to gender affirming healthcare because they did not fit a sufficiently binary presentation of gender. Non-binary people have reported feeling misunderstood by clinicians at gender clinics, who frame their experiences as binary, and consequently do not receive care that is suited to their needs. This leads non-binary people to adjust the healthcare they get to fit a more binary model, giving a more binary narrative of their gender in order to access the affirming care that they need, or go without healthcare altogether (Lykens et al., 2018).

Erasure of non-binary people can also come from within trans communities. Some trans people subscribe to the idea of *transmedicalism* which frames trans identity as a purely medical condition and often entails the denial of non-binary identity and the insistence that only binary trans people with lifelong dysphoria and a desire to undergo physical and social transition are 'truly' trans. The promotion of this idea can contribute to non-binary people feeling that they are not trans 'enough' and that they do not belong in trans spaces.

Identity exploration

Identity exploration is something that many trans people seek support with at some point in their transition. Non-binary people have the additional challenge of not having an established gender template to compare themselves against or work towards. In exploring and expressing our gender identities, we are carving out new spaces for ourselves in a binary society.

Through creating a non-judgemental environment, therapy can offer non-binary clients the opportunity to explore their identities in a way which feels safe. This could take the form of trying out new names, pronouns, identity labels, clothing and other forms of gender expression. While it is important that exploration is led by the client, it can be useful for the therapist to be informed about different gender identities so that they can provide information to help clients navigate their feelings.

Identity exploration, particularly for non-binary identities, may feel nebulous at times and this may evoke anxiety in either the client or therapist and a desire for certainty. It is important to recognise this when it happens. Through naming it and reiterating that there is no deadline for figuring out one's gender, therapists can act as stabilisers, holding the space and allowing the client to make sense of their feelings. Therapists should be careful to check their own desire for certainty so that they do not impose this onto clients. To come to the end of therapy without the client having arrived at a gender identity label should not necessarily be considered a negative outcome. Some people are OK with not knowing.

A few points to consider when working with non-binary people:

- While there is no research on the outcome of different psychological interventions for non-binary people (Scandurra et al., 2019), it is recommended that any form of therapy should take account of Minority Stress Theory (Meyer, 1995) and the role of social stigma, erasure and discrimination on mental health (Pipkin, 2021).
- Witnessing and affirming a client's non-binary gender can be significant for those who are unable to have their identities acknowledged elsewhere. Therapy can provide a space in which the dominant narratives about gender, including the pathologisation of marginalised identities, are challenged (Matsuno & Budge, 2017).
- Therapy can empower non-binary people through recognising the beauty and diversity of our identities and consider what it is that we may enjoy or appreciate about them.
- Through therapy, non-binary people may be supported to receive peer support by connecting with local or online LGBTQ+ communities, which is known to be beneficial for mental health and is associated with decreased depression and anxiety (Budge et al., 2014).
- Therapists should consider how some psychotherapeutic modalities, and the research upon which they draw, may frame and reinforce gender as binary. For a thorough review of the relationship between different modalities and the gender binary, see Barker and Iantaffi (2017).
- Therapeutic practices can be made more inclusive of non-binary people through the use of gender-neutral language, having non-binary options on forms which ask for gender, and ensuring that toilets are gender neutral.
- On a wider scale, we can all advocate for non-binary people through ensuring that the correct language is used for non-binary people in our day-to-day lives, through learning and educating others about non-binary identity, and by supporting the legal recognition of non-binary people.

Closing thoughts

The entire breadth and depth of the non-binary experience cannot be contained within one chapter. There is much more that could be said and I would encourage you to continue your learning through exploring the work of other non-binary writers, musicians, artists, speakers and activists from a variety of backgrounds and cultures.

In their own words: non-binary identities

'In their own words' is a collection of interviews of community members carried out by Skye. Here you can read their stories, unadulterated and directly from them. To learn more about the process, review the Preface.

I interviewed Alex (they/she) and Kay (they/he) about their experiences of being non-binary. Alex is a transfeminine non-binary person and Kay is an agender person. Here are extracts from our interview together.

Gender exploration and transition

Identity

Kay: *Being able to identify as non-binary is liberating for me, because I don't have to necessarily change who I am to feel comfortable about my gender.*

Social interactions

Alex: *I find that it's easier for me to connect with people sincerely. I feel like I don't need to articulate how I'm feeling through a specific register that might be acceptable in social circles as to how guys can talk about their feelings. That's something that I spend less time thinking about.*

Dating and relationships

Alex: *I feel like romantic and sexual relationships come with a lot more risk. I feel like a lot of men aren't open about liking queer people. It's very difficult finding someone who is both interested in you sexually and wants to be your friend. In terms of dating women, that's not really something that I feel safe doing at the moment because there's a lot of stereotypes out there about consent and trans people and how transfeminine people are just sneakily trying to trick their way into sleeping with women. There's a lot of negative press out there and that filters down into personal relationships and how I relate to the people close to me.*

Hormones

Alex: *Taking hormones in my experience has changed the physiological sensation of how I process emotions and that has made it easier to acknowledge when I'm feeling something and respond to that.*

Challenges

Living in a binary society

Kay: *Literally anytime you need to make a binary decision about some-thing, like where to go for a wee, or which changing rooms to use, even buying clothes. I wear men's underwear and I've taken some up to the till before in [high street retailer] and the cashier said, 'This is men's underwear, right?' First of all, I could fully be buying it for somebody else. Also, if I wanna wear men's underwear, I'll wear men's underwear …. I feel like the main challenge of being non-binary is other people just insisting that you pick a binary so often.*

Alex: *I'm doing a course at the moment at uni and this person was doing research about how knowing English as a second language affects your academic performance. And the first question they asked is, 'Are you a man or a woman?' And it's what are you really asking me? Are you asking me about my hormone balance? Do you think that this is a variable that is gonna be interesting in your research? Are you asking about how I was socialised? Are you asking me about how I socialise now? What is it that you're actually asking me? It wasn't very clear so I didn't really know how to answer that, but a binary was there.*

Gender neutral spaces

Kay: *I've always experienced a lot of misgendering when it comes to public toilets. The other week we were camping. I went into the ladies' show-ers and an old man said, 'That's the ladies.' I was feeling very exposed at the time and he still misgendered me. My knee jerk reaction was, 'I am a lady,' and then pushed my boobs at him, then obviously went into the shower and messaged all my queer group chats. 'What the fuck did I just do? I don't know why I did that. Am I trans enough?' I was having a meltdown of like, when I've had top surgery, what do I do when that happens? Do I just go in the men's? I don't know what to do.*

Legal recognition

Kay: *Where I work is very good with trans stuff and I can have Mx as my title. However, my pension provider defaults Mx to Mr so all of my* *pension stuff is Mr and I'm like, is this gonna be a problem if I die? Because legally, I'm not actually Mr.*

Alex: *I'm not really sure how much of the state involvement I need for me to be protected. On the one hand, why bother having Mx or any other letter specifying that on your passport? But the flip side of that is that I work in education and it's nice having the law protecting me that says that I'm not crazy ... schools are incredibly gendered places. Everyone's either a miss or a Mr or a Mrs and it's like, why is that important? Are you gonna treat someone who is a Ms with more or less respect based on that title? This is why I've resolved to get a PhD, because doctors are gender neutral.*

Healthcare

Kay: *Bad experiences I've had medically have been things like going for a smear. We got onto the questions that they ask you before your smear: are you sexually active? I said, 'I am but not with men.' And she said you don't need to have a smear. She was just so awkward about doing it. I dunno if she thought I was gonna be aroused by this horrific medical procedure she was gonna do on me, but that just made the whole thing awful and I don't wanna go for another one. And I think that the way that I present my gender and the fact that I don't have sex with men made that awkward.*

6 What about the parents?

Soon after I started working at adult gender specialist services, I realised how, when it comes to supporting gender-diverse people over the age of 18, parents and families (by birth, adoption or choice) are barely considered. Overall, the lack of resources forces professionals to focus on the individual, neglecting a systemic view of their circumstances and very sadly, often failing to provide safe spaces for families to ask questions, find support and accurate information. My private practice has granted me the freedom to create such spaces, and the following chapter reflects on what I have observed when meeting with parents of trans and non-binary folk.

No matter the age, most parents refer to their children as my 'child', 'daughter' or 'son'. However, when it comes to gender-diverse people, these terms might be inaccurate. Firstly, because the so-called 'child' might be 30 years old, and secondly, because the 'son' or 'daughter' might be non-binary. For the lack of more accurate terms and to mirror parents' voices, you might see me using the neutral term 'child' to talk about adult children. And I will use the terms 'daughter' and 'son' with single quotations to signal that parents are describing their child's birth assigned sex, as opposed to their gender identity.

Who we hoped our children would become

I put on two pairs of socks, two pairs of gloves, my motorbike gear and helmet, and I bravely stepped out to a freezing January morning. Even though it all sounded rather mystical, I ventured towards and joined the *Learning Through Dreams* Conference. The topic attracted a small crowd. I wasn't sure what to expect, as even though plenty is known about the neurological activity of the brain during sleep, the realm of dreams mostly remains a mystery. Psychoanalysis has studied them for over a century, attempting to extract meaning from these experiences. It has been postulated that they represent our inner demons and desires, that dreams are a natural recycling process of the brain and even that they are valuable exhibits of the collective unconscious.

The conference presented a variety of activities, undoubtedly the 'dream matrix' was the jewel in the crown. The largest room in the building housed about a hundred people who, creating the shape of a spiral, sat together. We were briefed to share any dreams we liked and, without order, one by one, people started to volunteer dreams of a jumbled nature. Uninstructed, we arrived at a relatable theme and rather abruptly the pace picked up. A woman declared, 'Even though I am over 70 and long ago went through the menopause, I often dream that I am pregnant.' Someone else said, 'I dreamt that I was going into labour, but the baby was made of jelly and because I could not hold it without dropping it, it lived inside a bucket by my bed.' A man shared, 'My partner has had many miscarriages, and sometimes I dream that I get to meet the unborn babies.' Someone else said, 'I dreamt that I lost my child in the park and spent the night searching for her.' Pregnancy, parenting and emotions of loss and fear towards real or imagined children were at the core of this group. One could say that they were at the centre of its collective unconscious.

When does anyone become a parent? Is it the first time they dream or imagine themselves in the role? Perhaps, it is when they first lay eyes on their children, or when their baby finally mumbles 'dada'. And how soon do expectations about what the child would look like, sound like and be like emerge? Some have been dreaming about it all their lives, creating elaborated fantasies about parenthood and about how perfect their children would be. Expectant parents are frequently asked, 'Are you hoping for a boy or a girl?' but we rarely delve deeper into what is being projected onto the child's sex. Parents build a psychological image of their children based on what they culturally believe their gender to be (Eccles et al., 1990; Weisgram & Bruun, 2018; Zamperini et al., 2016). For instance, if you are a mother and you are hoping for a girl, is this about having a female companion, overruling the patriarchy or buying all the Barbies you didn't get?

When gender-diverse folk come out to their parents, this experience often breaks fantasies which have been brewing for long before the child's birth. Surprisingly, many parents are bewildered when they realise that, in spite of their desires, children are people in their own right, with personalities, interests and behaviours that cannot always be traced back to their parents. Outrageously, this includes even having ownership of their own body and gender identity.

Assimilating the news

Influenced by their own intersectional identity, families vary in their view and reinforcement of traditional gender models. Their culture, socio-economic status, political ideology and others will affect the ease or challenge with which they assimilate that one of their members is gender or sexually diverse. In a spectrum, you can find at one end parents who tell you, 'This has been an absolute surprise to me. Ian plays rugby, has a beautiful muscular body and a girlfriend. How can this be?' On the other end, you might hear something like, 'I could always tell that Sophie was not interested in dolls. She often begged me to cut her hair short and questioned why she could not pee standing up.'

The issue is that not everyone has a typical gender development, so although there might be more clues in Sophie's story, that doesn't mean that Ian's gender feelings are less real – perhaps his struggle was hidden from view as he fought hard to fit in. Also, people can become aware of their gender identity at any point in their lives. The earliest is likely to be around the age of 5, once having acquired sufficient verbal skills to express their feelings and the latest – well there is no age limit. Individuals above the age of 50 tend to be well aware of their gender feelings for decades before they decide to come out and crucial life events such as death of parents, separation from a partner or children leaving home tend to precipitate their transition.

Needless to say, even in the presence of evident clues hinting that someone is exploring or struggling with their gender identity, parents might decide to overlook the issue. Some, filled with worry, hope that this 'phase' will go away, whereas others are just not sure how to approach the topic. After all, having a trans identity poses added challenges to life and parents often worry about a whole range of things: discrimination and safety, the long-term effects of the hormones, the journey to self-acceptance and, what I most frequently hear, 'Will they come to regret it?' We address some of these worries in Chapter 4, *Arriving at the right decision.*

The burdensome weight of traditions

Body modifications are practised all around the world. They perpetuate tradition, enhance group cohesiveness, comply with beauty standards and are even used as means of control. Some examples are female genital mutilation, scarification or tooth sharpening. In the pursuit of expanding my understanding of this topic, I watched the documentary *American Circumcision* (Marotta, 2017). Up until that stage, I thought that male circumcision was only practised due to medical or religious reasons. Unlike what I thought, there is a great variability by country. For example, 80.5 per cent of North Americans are circumcised (Introcaso et al., 2013; Morris et al., 2014); in comparison to 15 to 20 per cent of British men (Dave, 2003). There is a lot of misinformation surrounding the topic, and circumcision has been thought to protect from sexually transmitted diseases such as HIV and to be prophylactic against infection (though surely washing regularly would be equally effective and less painful). Currently, the main driving force to perpetuate this practice is what society considers to be a normal-looking penis. And, reviewing these numbers, it seems like in the US nobody wants to be singled out in the changing room for being uncircumcised.

So, what are the consequences of circumcision? Research has established that through the exposure of the glans, the penis loses sensitivity as its skin is forced to harden, ultimately reducing sexual pleasure. So, in the case of non-religious practices, where there are no medical conditions (such as phimosis) to require it, and knowing that it can reduce sexual pleasure, why do 80.5 per cent of Americans parents opt for it? The documentary poses an interesting argument which is that, for a future generation of Americans to retain their foreskin, the current generation would need to admit that something was done to their body without their consent, resulting in permanent changes to its structure and potentially hindering its function. The current generation of Americans would have to realise that it was their own parents who robbed them of a choice in the matter and that, in order not to repeat the same pattern, they would have to overcome the primordial narcissism that accompanies parenthood – one that drives them to hope that their children would be mini versions of themselves (penis included).

This might sound off-topic from the experience of parents of trans people, but to me it bears some commonalities. Firstly, it speaks about the difficulty that cisgender parents experience when envisioning their children taking ownership of their own bodies and expressing bodily autonomy, as they can believe that their children's bodies rightfully belong to them. Secondly, it is to do with overcoming the challenge of thinking about their children's bodies with a different configuration from their own (and that of the majority of society). Lastly, this means questioning what it is and means to be a man or a woman, and how this might not be purely dictated by the appearance of your genitals. We inherit a certain view of the world, and some will do almost anything to perpetuate it.

You don't know what it's like

When a parent learns that their (underage or adult) child is trans, many go through what in literature has been defined as an *ambiguous loss*. The term refers to the emotions of loss associated to the gender-diverse person being present, while their cisgender male or female gender identity is grieved by the parent (Coolhart et al., 2018; McGuire et al., 2016; Norwood, 2013; Riggs & Bartholomaeus, 2018). In this section, we will use the Kübler-Ross five stages of grief model to frame these feelings. You might have seen this model mostly associated with the death of a loved one but, in this instance, we will adapt it to the loss of a cisnormative familial identity when coming to accept the dissolution of gender projections placed on the children. Please consider that these are non-sequential stages.

Denial

This becomes apparent in cases when the gender-diverse person has come out, yet the topic becomes the elephant in the room. Gender is no longer addressed or acknowledged, almost as if the conversation didn't happen. Parents avoid asking follow-up questions or showing curiosity about what is to come next in terms of gender exploration and transition. As Buxton (2006) said, '[E]ven in an accepting family, the disclosure often involves shock, disbelief, confusion, and loss'.

Anger

In this step, parents recognise that the disclosure cannot be perpetually ignored. This forced confrontation with their new reality can increase frustration and an emotional disconnect between parent and children. Some parents can become upset at their child, presuming that they are doing this as a form of rebellion. Others might be resentful towards families who seemingly have it easier. A few might anticipate the loss of never becoming a grandparent, wondering 'What have I done to deserve this?'. Parents might try and search for someone or something to blame their child's diversity on, often their peers and the media are pointed to as the sources of information and precipitants of gender exploratory thoughts. Most recently, as one of my adult clients came out to her parents, in response to this disclosure, her mother alluded to a conspiracy theory, formulating that the microplastics in the ocean are the reason for increased levels of oestrogen in individuals assigned male at birth, causing them to identify as trans women. (I mean, how do you respond to that?) It is not unusual to undergo a period of adjustment whereby a pattern of distancing and deterioration might be observed, followed by gradual return to improvement (Laird, 1996; Savin-Williams, 1996), and so time and patience are a valid approach.

Bargaining

Sometimes parents attempt to negotiate elements of their children's transition. For example, suggesting that their 'son' commits to dressing in a somewhat feminine fashion, but not identifying as female. As a stepping stone, some families start by using neutral nicknames and 'they/them' pronouns, as opposed to those linked to a binary identity. Some parents might suggest deadlines to delay their child's transition, for example, 'I will support you in accessing hormone therapy once you graduate from university.' Others might call their child by their chosen name and pronouns but draw the line at affirming or supporting decisions around surgery. And, as younger adults are less likely to have the economic independence to pursue interventions on their own, they might view these stances as means of control.

Depression

Underneath depression there lies a variety of emotions. Shame surfaces with lingering questions like: 'What will I say to my friends when they ask me about my daughter?' Some struggle with guilt, worrying that they did something wrong that caused their child to be trans, and even expect fingers to be pointed at them for being bad parents. Anticipating that they will not be accepted, parents might end up distancing themselves from their social or spiritual communities, ultimately, increasing isolation and self-perceived defectiveness. The inability to control the changes brought up by transition can increase feelings of helplessness, promoting circular patterns between the stages of depression and bargaining. Also, within traditional family structures formed by parental couples, there might be disagreements and disparities in the way of dealing with having a trans child. This can prompt communication difficulties, conflict and splitting where one parent is supportive and the other one is not.

Acceptance

Sadly, not everyone reaches this stage. But time, information, support, open conversations and ultimately a desire to have a relationship with their children can help a great deal. During this stage parents accept that their child is trans or non-binary and feel like, although their diversity might pose challenges, perhaps it is not as bad as they initially anticipated. You might hear comments like, 'Although it would have been easier if my child was cisgender, I ought to accept who they are.' Testoni and Pinducciu (2019) did a thematic analysis of the experiences of parents of trans people, finding that within the phase of 'mourning, orientation and restoration' what helped most was to understand that they had not lost their children, but an imaginary version of them, having challenged preconceptions and transphobia, and lastly, having understood that their child can be trans and happy.

Feelings of concern towards the psychological and physical safety of one's child can be channelled onto finding ways to produce positive changes in their environment. For example, in the case of children who are in education, parents can campaign for schools to be inclusive, creating anti-bullying policies, facilitating information around diversity, creating inclusive spaces like toilets and changing rooms, and discouraging teachers from promoting gender divisions through separating students by gender. Family acceptance is crucial for cisgender and gender-diverse people, and studies have shown how young transgender folk who have been rejected by their families suffer lesser life satisfaction, psychological health and lower self-esteem levels (Rotondi et al., 2011).

Food for thought: Transitioning in Poland

As you would have learned by now, when a gender-diverse person transitions, they go through a multi-layered process of change. Among many others, trans people might wish to formalise their gender identity by changing legal documents such as passports to the correct name and gender. This process is different in each country, and the Polish government is rather special. In 2022, trans individuals wishing to have their identity recognised sought to pursue a civil lawsuit against their parents for having wrongly identified their gender as the one corresponding to their birth-assigned sex.

- Consider what kind of underlying message the government sends to those families. What dynamic elicits saying to your parents 'not only am I trans, but I have to take you to court'? How may the trans person, their parents, and those witnessing this event end up feeling about it?

Two sides of the same coin

Working as a gender-specialist, particularly when the trans or non-binary person is our primary client, we are inclined to see their side of the story. Therapists want to be understanding and sometimes, unbeknown to us, we might fail to connect with the parent's position. Menvielle & Rodnan (2011) found that when mental health professionals helped and encouraged parents to be affirming, as opposed to pathologising their responses, this increased their ability to be supportive.

In 2019, I was invited to deliver a talk at Free2Be Alliance, a London LGBTQI+ organisation supporting young people and their families. Parents were invited to voice their emotions around their children's transition and unexpectedly, a mother asked me a question that up until this day stays with me. 'Laura,' she said, 'What do I do with the pictures? My son asked me to remove every photo from before he came out and started to present in male role. I have boxes full of them, and a hidden folder on my laptop. I sometimes look at them, at what 'she' – I mean he – looked like. My son does not let me hang them anymore, but I do not have the heart to throw them away.'

My heart sank and I was left with a mirrored feeling of helplessness. To me, this mother was not only grieving the loss of a 'daughter', but the loss of the child she had, as he distanced himself further into adolescence and adulthood. Parents often look with nostalgia at the years when their children were younger, potentially a time when there were fewer family conflicts, and when they had a greater sense of control. Letting go of the 'daughter' can therefore be understood as just as important as letting go of their childhood and the implications and meanings made of that child–adult relationship.

Exercise

How would *you* help this mother process her feelings of loss?
Here are a few suggestions:

- Normalising her feelings
- Supporting a mutual understanding by which she could empathise with her son's dysphoria when seeing his earlier life pictures, and supporting the son in empathising with his mother's love for all stages of his life (regardless of what he looked like)
- Negotiating with her son for a place where the pictures might be able to live

---

Sometimes, family members come to therapy with different agendas. On the one hand, you might find parents hoping that the trans child changes their mind; and on the other, the trans person hoping for acceptance. As Pearlman (2006) describes, therapists inhabit two contradictory empathic locations: firstly, sympathising with the parents' feelings; and secondly, being a compassionate and knowledgeable advocate for the trans child, understanding both sides and thus facilitating adjustment and reconciliation.

Conflict commonly arises when, during family sessions, there is misgendering. Ella and her father James came to the session hoping to work through their relationship and frequent arguing. Ella, who identifies as trans female, asked me to use 'she/her' pronouns. This explicit request was not heard by her father, however, and, as James started to talk, he consistently referred to Ella by the name of 'Matt' and used 'he/him' pronouns. I observed Ella's facial expressions and reactions to misgendering, at times, met with silence, and at others with a sigh of despair or an occasional correction. On more than one occasion I have been in this predicament, pondering, is it my place to correct the parent, and does Ella hope that I'd do this for her? I waited a couple of times to see if her dad realised his mistake, and, as it seemed this was intentional, I said, 'I have noticed that you continue to address Ella by her birth name and pronouns, can you tell me a little bit more about this?' This question sometimes triggers an apology and a better attempt to get it right; sometimes the person may simply say, 'I did not know I should also be doing this,' but often it uncovers a variety of reasons for resistance, like:

* 'I have been calling him Matt for 20 years. I cannot be expected to suddenly change.'
* 'When he starts looking more feminine, I will start calling him Ella.'
* 'It is hard for me to say this name. It is too early.'
* 'This gender thing is only a phase.'

Some parents might be posed with the dilemma as to how affirming they should be, worrying that if they are to call their (underage or adult) child by their chosen name, they might be encouraging them to transition, whereas if they refuse, this might discourage them or make them think more carefully. It is interesting to explore perceived parental values and obligations with parents; for instance, is it your duty as a parent to always accept and love your child? And should you always protect your child (even from themselves)? What tends to be omitted is that misgendering can trigger a great sense of discomfort and shame for trans folk. This repeated experience when around one's parents can precipitate a rupture of the relationship, whereby the trans person feels unsupported, disrespected and unseen.

Hurt and abuse from family members

Gender-diverse people experience *identity-related abuse* (Riggs et al., 2016; Rogers, 2017), a term that refers to experiences of abuse in relation to gender and gender presentation. Some forms of abuse include denying a person's trans identity, commenting negatively about their body or appearance, threatening to 'out them' (to reveal their trans identity to others without their consent), intentionally misgendering them, or withholding economic means so that they cannot access gender-affirming interventions. A large survey in the US (N = 27,715) composed of adult gender-diverse people found that 1 in 10 reported violence from family members (James et al., 2016). Nuttbrock et al. (2010) extracted a sub-sample (N = 571) of transgender women from the previous study, concluding that 78.1 per cent reported psychological abuse at some stage of their lives, most often during adolescence and coming from parents or other family members.

It is important to acknowledge that not many parents set out to be unsupportive of their children – most battle their emotions and try to help and love their children no matter what. However, even though most do not intend to hurt them, it is not intention but actions that prevent the harm. If you observe that your client is at risk, collaboratively design a safety plan to help them prevent or escape abuse. If you observe these behaviours or attitudes in parents – with compassion – challenge them.

In their own words: meet the parents

'In their own words' is a collection of interviews of community members carried out by Skye. Here you can read their stories, unadulterated and directly from them. To learn more about the process, review the Preface.

For the past couple of years, Laura has been providing an annual talk and reflective space for Families Together London. This support group provides a space for the parents of LGBTQI+ people to come together, share their experiences and support one another. In recent years, the number of parents of trans and non-binary folk who have joined the group has grown tremendously. We reached out to the group, inviting members to be interviewed about their experiences for our book. Michael (he/him), Anna (she/her), and Eve (she/her) responded saying they would like to take part. Here are extracts from my conversation with them. Initials and pseudonyms have been used to protect the identity of the interviewees and that of their children.

Response to coming out

Anna: *I was disbelieving I have to say. It was just before she did her GCSEs and I seem to remember trying to put it on hold and not talk about it for a little while. It came completely out of the blue, obviously not to her but to us, yeah.*

Eve: *If I tell you that I was absolutely devastated, it's not an understatement. There was no indication whatsoever, but she was quite withdrawn and had been since the end of school. She said she can't look back and say that's how she always felt, but she had come to this conclusion. I found it really hard.*

Challenges

Discussing transition

Michael: *I think for me it's the challenge of having a conversation about transgender and the whys, the wherefores, and where do you think this is going for you, that kind of thinking or questioning is extremely difficult with our younger one. It's a conversation you can't have in a way.*

Effect on the wider family

Eve: *I did contact my family and one half were, 'Okay, we'll just have to
         adjust to that. That's fine.' And others were, 'No. What do you mean?
         Have you tried speaking to her? This can't be right,' and were very
         dismissive. It was really disappointing.*

Anxiety

Michael: *Over time, as a parent, you accommodate to the change in your
         child. At the same time there will always be some anxiety. There's
         a process of adapting to change, but at the same time, things are
         never going to be the same. And it's how you just go on living with
         that. I guess that's life, isn't it? And quite apart from transgender
         issues, other people have kids who, I don't know, they're gay or they
         just go off on a different career that's not what you might have
         hoped for as a parent or, they end up having mental health issues
         or addiction. We're not alone in the world as a group of parents
         fretting about their children but the relationship is the most
         important thing of all.*

Effect on friendships

Anna: *And it does feel like sometimes, when I speak to my friends, I feel
         as though they don't necessarily want to ask me about it. It's the
         elephant in the room and then you feel as though it's a bit of
         your life that you can't be as open as you would want to be. Not
         that I'm not open about it but actually you can't because they
         don't get it.*

Support

Anna: *Just being able to listen to people who understand what you're
         going through, although I've got very good friends who I can
         speak to, they just don't get it. And there is grief. There is abso-
         lutely grief and there is also pride, I have to say. I'm really proud
         of her... It's always helpful to talk about it. It makes you think
         about it in a slightly different way. I think you can get a bit
         wrapped up in yourself and your own thoughts and actually
         that's never good.*

Eve: *I found the group absolutely amazing. I was put in touch with
         somebody who was a parent of a trans child whose situation
         sounded very similar to mine. It was a lifeline really to find some-
         body. It took me a long time to find anybody to give me the support
         I needed, who understood what I was feeling.*

Healthcare

Michael: *I would say adequate mental health support for a lot of teenagers and then subsequently young adults is not that great. When he went to university, he decided he'd go and see his local GP and get referred for hormones and was on the waiting list for ages and ages, and then moved back to London. In the end we just said let's refer you privately and that's how he got his hormones .... If you couldn't afford to go private it's one hell of a wait and it's got worse.*

Anna: *So Alice was referred to a psychiatrist, then a psychologist and was put on the waiting list for the gender identity clinic four-and-a-half years ago. There have been times when we've paid. We can afford to pay, but actually it's just not on. It's awful. The first appointment was by telephone in October. So it was four years later. We've had one appointment since then. We're still waiting for an endocrinologist. So, in the end, because Alice is now getting desperate, she is going to be prescribed private hormones which is good for her, but actually it's just appalling.*

Political climate

Michael: *The other issue is the social aspect and the politicisation of it ... You worry about their safety out there in the world and, depending on where they're going out to.*

Anna: *Every time I open the paper ... it just gets my goat. I don't know what it is with the media at the moment. They just seem to be out for trans people right now. Just leave them alone.*

Eve: *Are you like me? You zone in on it now?*

Anna: *Yeah, and I have to be in the right mood. I have to just skip it cause otherwise I'm upset for the rest of the day. It's just not fair.*

Eve: *It's the next group of people to bash, isn't it?*

Anna: *Yes. I think it's also about understanding. I didn't know a lot about trans people before I have to say. So some of it is education.*

7 Sexuality, romance and identity labels

Sex is one the largest industries in the world, the driver of many passions and sometimes a source of shame and embarrassment. It is interesting to think about the relationship that we all form with sex and sexuality and, to do so, we ought to look back at our own history and at how this concept of 'the birds and the bees' was communicated to us, if at all. Perhaps you first came across it when peering through your neighbour's window, or a friend showed you a bewildering porn site; maybe it was the suggestion of a sex scene in a PG-rated movie that, with a touch of the remote, your father instantly censored.

The first time I was formally introduced to sex, it was merged with the concept of gender, love and reproduction. All Year 4 students were called to an assembly, to which parents were also invited. Children sat at the front and adults at the back. Once everyone settled, a priest started the talk, illustrating his ideas with the cutting-edge technology of the analogue era – the slide projector. Showing us an image of an athlete of gender-neutral appearance, the priest assertively asked us, 'Is this a man, or a woman?' A mixture of giggles and silence filled the air. In a room full of confused children, no one dared to point to the athlete's apparent breasts. I must admit, the rest of the talk is a bit of a blur. I assume that we were told about men and women's bodies, and we must have been provided with some encoded reference to penetration. It all ended with an invitation to run and thank our parents for 'the gift of life'. Bizarre. During adolescence, we engaged with sex education. We learned to keep our virginity until marriage, about contraception, periods and venereal diseases. Nobody ever mentioned the slight possibility of pleasure, even as a side effect of sex. Nobody told us about intimacy, touch, taste or roles. Needless to say, consent, sexting or social media weren't part of the agenda. And only embarrassingly late I learnt more about other forms of non-vanilla, penis-in-vagina sex.

A moment for reflection

- When was the first time you became aware of sex?
- What platform facilitated this information? (i.e., movie, porn magazine, school, your siblings, your parents)
- What sort of emotions are attached to this memory?
- Did you learn about LGBTQI+ people and other forms of pleasure?

These are not only questions to ask yourself, but also to ask your clients. They will help you understand what embedded feelings surround the topic, and if their perception of sex has evolved.

Sex in the therapy room

In therapy, there is always a moment of silence, a second of choking embarrassment that speaks louder than words. Many do not know how to approach the conversation; they hesitate, whirl around it and even ask for permission to open Pandora's box. Sexuality can be a hairy subject for both practitioners and clients. It has always surprised me that in healthcare settings this is not explored with the frequency or ease that it should. Sexual function is no different from sleep, concentration, eating or elimination (i.e., defecation or urination), so why do practitioners struggle to ask about it? I wonder if some therapists worry about prying, eliciting erotic transference or simply not knowing what to do once their questions are answered.

> ### A question for you
>
> Perhaps this is a good moment for you to think about your current workload. With how many of your clients have you explored sexuality? And by this I mean not only sexual orientation, but also their levels of sexual drive, masturbation habits and whether they find sex pleasurable and/or reach orgasm in sex.

These questions, as personal as they might seem, help us to map the person's ability to feel pleasure, which is closely associated with their mental health. At a global level, the rates of depression and anxiety have risen since the pandemic and now, one in every three people experience these conditions (Salari et al., 2020). Based on these numbers, how many of your clients do you think might be struggling with their sexual life? And how many of them do you think would be proactive in talking about it? When approaching sexuality (as well as most issues) we benefit from using an intersectional frame, as depending on the person's age, culture or gender, sexuality can be a particularly taboo topic. Through addressing these issues, we can unveil the connection (or lack thereof) to their body, their self-esteem and positioning in relation to their partner. For example, is their partner's pleasure more important than their own? And is this a reflection of their overall relationship dynamics? So, if you haven't done so already, what is stopping you from asking?

Sexual identity labels

The concepts of sexuality and gender identity are often interlinked and confused. This is not by design, but due to cisnormative and heteronormative models of understanding human identity and desire. Many belonging to sexual and gender minorities have united forces in the acronym LGBTQI+, forming inclusive spaces and advocating for equality, although, not all sexually diverse communities are accepting of gender-diverse people, and there are subgroups who exclude trans and non-binary folk.

Currently, most people are only aware of a few sexualities, such as heterosexual, lesbian or gay, and bisexual. The issue with these identities is that they are built on the premise that one is attracted to the 'opposite sex', the 'same sex', or 'both sexes'. Therefore, in some cases this model might not be applicable to individuals with trans or non-binary identities, as gender and sexed bodies would not neatly correlate. For example, based on these categorisations, would a trans woman who has retained her penis and testicles, and has a female (cisgender) partner self-define as a lesbian when they occasionally have penis-in-vagina intercourse? This will depend on the individual's self-perception; some people in the above scenario might identify with the term lesbian, others with 'queer', and some might avoid labels as a whole. Also, some of the traditional sexual orientation labels might not accurately describe the sexuality of a non-binary person attracted to male partners. This is because trans and non-binary folk can have non-normative body configurations, or not identify as strictly male or female. This is why we must check with our clients what words best describe their attraction to others.

So, aside from the bodies of the two (or multiple people) involved in the act, what other elements could be used to define sexual pleasure? Individuals within the kink, bondage, or BDSM communities might not be limited by the sex of the person with whom they are sharing a scene, but their attraction is often linked to power, role play or sensation. Generally, some people might be particularly attracted towards androgyny, whereas others get a kick out of receiving oral sex. In both and many other cases they might be disregarding what body the individual occupies or how they identify. This is because sexuality can comprise broad elements like sensation, body, partner, power dynamics, love, vulnerability, consent, pleasure, risk, intelligence and spirituality (Bornstein, 2013).

As people come to understand their desire beyond binary boxes, a myriad of sexual identity labels appear, such as the term *sapiophile*, which refers to being sexually or romantically attracted towards people with whom we form an intellectual bond. So, what are the most used LGBTQI+ labels? The National LGBT Survey Report (Government Equalities Office, 2018) stated the prevalence in sexual identifications from a sample of 100,000 LGBTQ people in the UK, finding that 61 per cent identified as lesbian or gay, 26 per cent as bisexual, 4 per cent as pansexual, 2 per cent as asexual, 1 per cent as queer, and 6 per cent were undetermined. Particularly for members of sexual minorities groups, apart from denoting attraction, sexual orientation also relates to political ideology, struggles and community memberships (Kuper et al., 2012; Twist, 2017).

A minority within a minority

Being a minority within a minority brings its own set of challenges, and individuals with pansexual, bisexual, asexual, kink or polyamorous identities might be subject to greater stereotypes, discrimination and psychological distress than those with more traditional sexual identities. For this reason, I wanted to pay a little bit of extra attention to them.

Pansexuality refers to the romantic or sexual attraction towards individuals, irrespective of their gender identity or body configuration. This term is frequently linked to that of bisexuality, although the latter tends to limit attraction towards women or men (occasionally excluding gender-diverse people). Interestingly, it seems like non-binary people often identify as pansexual, as their identity and desire does not seem to be constrained by binaries. Kuper et al. (2012) studied an online sample of 292 gender-diverse people, mostly composed of non-binary folk, concluding that 'pansexual' and 'queer' were the most commonly used sexual identity labels. Similarly, my colleagues and I carried out a study of 189 non-binary people seeking support at the NHS Gender Identity Clinic in Charing Cross (London), where 46 per cent of our sample described being attracted towards multiple genders and, unexpectedly, 18.6 per cent of our sample self-defined as asexual (Evans et al., 2019).

Asexuality can be misunderstood and omitted as a form of sexual orientation. It refers to the lack of interest or desire to have sexual encounters with oneself and/or others. Sometimes, the origin of this identification might be linked to biological components, such as reduced testosterone levels in individuals with a male phenotype, but biology is not necessarily linked to asexuality. It is the result of diversity, and it is not defective in its nature. Some asexual people have romantic relationships and might self-define as, for instance, 'asexual panromantic' (this is to say, interested in having romantic relationships with multiple genders, but no sex). Asexuality works as an umbrella term and, within it, there are broad ways of identifying. Within the general British population, it is estimated that 1 per cent of people are asexual (Bogaert, 2004; Herman, 2016), however the rates seem to be higher within gender-diverse groups. Herman (2016) studied a sample of 6368 trans and non-binary people, finding a prevalence rate of asexuality of 4 per cent. In the same study, the rates of asexuality in individuals assigned female at birth were twice those of people assigned male at birth. As gender-diverse folk frequently struggle with their relationship with their body, this can affect their wish to relate to themselves and to others sexually. Some trans and non-binary people who have physically transitioned and experience greater congruency and ease might find themselves experiencing increased libido. This is particularly prevalent in transmasculine identified people who, as a side effect of testosterone therapy, can experience increased sexual drive.

Lastly, I would like to mention relationship diversity, often referred to as *consensual non-monogamy, polyamory* and its other forms. In the west, coupledom and strict monogamy have been placed as society's gold standard. We have been indoctrinated to commit to 'the one', disregarding other forms of sexually and emotionally connecting to others. Most people follow the Church's rulebook (or whatever scripture you read) on how to love and have not stopped to question what would make them happy. Sadly, there are a lot of negative stereotypes and misinformation towards those who do not love and live in pairs. Open relationship arrangements sometimes come into the conversation for couples who are transitioning, as every aspect of their relationship gets re-evaluated. Relationship diversity can be present in cases where there is sexual dissatisfaction, or simply a desire to experience other forms of closeness with individuals outside the couple, all while staying together.

Transitioning together

Couples who transition together often face the challenge of redefining their community memberships. For instance, take a gay couple whose social support network is predominantly formed of gay men: if one of the members transitions to a female role, suddenly they would be seen and even treated as a straight couple. Their access to queer social spaces might be limited by others and/or themselves, and their identity as a couple belonging to a sexual minority group becomes invisible. For this reason, it is important to address with the non-transitioning partner how these social changes are experienced. Some partners take it as a normal part of transition, whereas others are filled with resentment for the sacrifices they feel they ought to make.

In transitioning as a couple, they might also live through a reconfiguration of their sexuality. Using the same example, the non-transitioning partner is gay and has always been attracted to men, so when his partner transitions to a female role, he might be confused as to whether he would find her attractive, as her name, voice, manners and even smell changes to embody femininity. The trans partner might propose renegotiating some of the existing sexual boundaries, suggesting that she will no longer feel comfortable with penetrating him. Additionally, legal changes can be made, as some countries require an authorisation from the non-transitioning spouse to re-validate their marriage, or for the couple to dissolve their marriage and later engage in a civil partnership.

When a non-transitioning partner becomes aware of their partner's trans identity, some might feel cheated and lied to; some spouses have mentioned feeling like they no longer know the person they married, experiencing guilt, embarrassment or even anger for not having noticed their partner's gender struggles. You are likely to observe changes in power dynamics. Some non-transitioning partners describe feeling drained as transition can occupy the space of many conversations, and as the trans partner might start paying a lot more attention to their own identity and needs. On occasion, the non-transitioning partner might take up the role of a carer, as the trans partner undergoes surgeries and interventions where emotional and practical support is required. As a result, the non-transitioning partner can start to self-perceive or be perceived by others as a bit of a 'saint' for facilitating transition. Some people might even pity the non-transitioning partner for shouldering changes outside of their control, and for coping with the potential discrimination and rejection of their communities.

Chicken or egg

As exemplified above, some gender-diverse people firstly become aware of their sexual identity, and later of their gender identity, consequently the label they use to define their sexuality might change in the process. But also, occasionally, sexual orientation can change following transition (Daskalos, 1998; Lawrence, 2005). For any one of us, sexual identity can shift and change during different periods of our lives, and so can the importance that we attribute to it. Broadly speaking, we would expect 18-years-olds to be more interested in sex than 84-year-olds. Also, it is common to experiment sexually during adolescence and early adulthood without necessarily identifying with a queer label. For example, would you say that a woman who, during university, had a few cheeky kisses with other women, but only formed relationships with men, is bisexual? Only that person can define their sexuality, and the parameters used will vary. Some people think that having the desire but not acting on it excludes them from identifying as such. As recorded in the documentary *Pray Away* (Stolakis, 2021), this is the case of the so-called 'reformed gays' who, through reparative therapy and praying, claim to have suppressed their same sex attraction. To many that's sufficient to self-define as straight. So, whatever sexual identity label your client uses, it is always worth going deeper into the meaning and definition of these labels.

When trans and non-binary people come to terms with their identity, change their presentation and modify their bodies, they get to see themselves in a different light. The boundaries of what made them feel dysphoric might change, and so might their desire. Many of us are bound to traditional ideas around how women should be passive in bed, thus being penetrated, and how men should be active in bed, therefore penetrating. So, even though many trans people are able to experience pleasure from using their genitals with a partner, the way in which they perceive themselves or are perceived by others can hinder this pleasure. For example, a trans man who has retained his vagina while having penetrative sex with a (cisgender) male partner, might be concerned that by being penetrated he is taking a traditional feminine position. This is because, in their identity and body configuration, trans men without genital surgery redefine social norms of masculinity and manhood (Green, 2020; Kotula, 2002; Vanderburgh, 2007). Having an open conversation with one's partner can often support changing these perceptions, increasing the enjoyment of sex. So, even though this trans man might be penetrated, he might feel reassured if his partner softly whispers in his ear, 'You look handsome and sexy.' When stepping outside of heteronormative ways of relating sexually, we come to find that a lot more open communication about our likes, dislikes, do's and don'ts is needed. You can normalise this process through supporting couples to create lists, sharing them and negotiating what scenes, body parts and dynamics would make them feel safe yet excited. And let's not forget that 'coping with intimacy, honesty, communication, and changing bodies over time are universal concerns' (Istarlev & Sennott, 2012, p. 122).

Is this a fetish or am I trans?

In the field of gender there is stigma attached to experiencing sexual arousal when presenting in a gender role different from that corresponding to one's birth assigned sex. Long ago these experiences were conceptualised as a type of sexual orientation and were defined by Blanchard (1989) as *autogynephilia* (referring to sexual pleasure in individuals assigned male at birth when presenting in female role) and by Lawrence (2007) as *autoandrophilia* (refer-ring to sexual pleasure in individuals assigned female at birth when presenting in male role). These concepts have been heavily criticised (Moser, 2009, 2010; Serano, 2020; Veale, 2015; Veale et al., 2008) as they pathologise the natural experience of sexual pleasure in gender-diverse people. In line with this, low sex drive used to be a criterion for diagnosis of 'transsexualism' (Lewins, 1995).

Interestingly, Moser (2009) studied the descriptors of autogynephilia in cis-gender women, asking them to rate the veracity of statements such as 'I have been erotically aroused by contemplating myself fully clothed in sexy attire', 'I have been erotically aroused by contemplating myself wearing lingerie', or by 'imagining myself with a sexier body'. I am not sure about you, but some of these accounts do resonate with my experience (as a cis woman). The results were astonishing, finding that 93 per cent of cisgender women would potentially meet the diagnosis for autogynephilia. These results do not deny the existence of individuals who have a purely sexual relationship with 'cross-dressing', but it certainly normalises sexual arousal in gender-diverse populations.

More than once clients have asked me, 'Is this a fetish or am I trans?' Let me share with you a few principles for exploration and, forgive me, as I have only encountered this dilemma with individuals assigned male at birth, thus, I will focus on the female-identifying population. Also, in my experience, these cases are rarer than one might think, only having worked with a handful of people who were truly troubled by this question. Instead, what I have found is that, as the media frequently portrays trans folk as sexual predators, some trans people are ashamed and afraid of their (completely normal) sexual desire.

Sexuality is an amalgamation between who I am and what I like, and sex can be a safe playground to explore one's identity, giving us permission to behave in ways that the outside world might find objectionable. So, in the case of clients who get sexual pleasure from presenting in female role, I wonder, are they using sex as a safe exploration ground for their gender identity, or is this exclusively about pleasure? If the latter resonated with them, we might frame this desire as a fetish, although this definition might not always apply.

Fetishes are rooted in the forbidden, the rare, the unattainable. They are the places one goes to feel excited and, if they start to become part of day-to-day life, then these places are likely to lose their exhilarating power. It is easier to feel aroused when alone, at home, gazing at one's body in lingerie, than when going to the supermarket to buy groceries and wearing sportswear. If wearing female lingerie arouses your client and they are only seeking this for sexual gratification, I would ask them to test the nature of their behaviour by present-ing in female role in a situation that is mundane, and, potentially, outside of their home environment. If your client extracted affirmation from being their female-self in a situation unrelated to sex, it might be that your client has a female identity. Also, I would wonder, does presenting in female role always lead to arousal? For example, has your client remained in female role after they have found sexual gratification, perhaps initially masturbating and later just watching TV? And, lastly, does your client see themselves as female in situations unrelated to sex, for example at work when talking with a group of all-female colleagues? If femininity is one-dimensional, this is to say it only exists in the context of sex, then it is likely that taking on a full-time female identity and transitioning might not be the right step for your client.

Dating as a trans person

Minority groups tend to be objectified and even sexualised by the masses. A person's ethnicity, sexual and gender identity or disability can ignite the lust of those with greater privilege, generally through dynamics of dominance and submissiveness. We are all familiar with widespread fantasies around Black men's larger penises and hyper sexualised nature, petite and compliant Asian women, or those fiery Latinos. All these discourses are evidently based on stereotypes that, through popular culture and the porn industry, continue to be reinforced.

To make these claims concrete I embarked on what I have found to be an enlightening read, porn analytics (PornHub, 2019). PornHub published an extensive list of most searched terms by country, sex differences, time of the day and other parameters. Minority sex groups like lesbians have steadily remained at the top of the most sought-after list. Although less prevalent in the mainstream fantasies, there is also 'disabled sex', where the struggle of individuals with disabilities is depicted as arousing, like in scenes where amputees come in and out of a wheelchair. Pertinent to our book, within this list we find 'transgender' as one of most searched terms. Having split these statistics based on the sex of the person searching for footage, we found that trans porn is featured as (presumably straight, cisgender) men's 12th most favourite type of porn.

So, what does this mean for trans and non-binary folk entering the dating scene? Many of my clients report being concerned about how and when to disclose their gender identity. Should this be part of their dating profile, or should they wait until meeting their date? Many fear rejection and also might conceive their trans identity as a small part of themselves, so why should it become the first thing another person learns about them? Some are concerned about their safety, and they might take extra steps towards protecting themselves, like telling a friend when, where and with whom they will meet.

The Netflix documentary *Disclosure* (Sam Feder, 2020) speaks about the portrayal of trans people in the media, and in a section, it references the popular narrative of how trans people 'trick cisgender people into being attracted to them'. To exemplify it, in the movie *Ace Ventura* (Shadyac, 1994) the main character played by Jim Carrey is revolted when realising that the woman he likes is trans, to such a degree, that he repeatedly vomits. Gender-diverse folk frequently worry that their identity or body configuration might cause disgust to others, and that they might be punished due to transphobia and homophobia.

A proportion of people worry about becoming a mere object of desire where who they are matters less than their genital configuration. This is, of course, assuming that the person is looking for a meaningful encounter or relationship, which is not always the case. Through sex, cisgender and gender-diverse people often seek to find validation of their attractiveness, desirability, masculinity or femininity. However, within trans and non-binary groups, seeking validation of one's gender identity through having sex with cisgender partners can lead to complex power plays that perpetuate the perceived superiority of cisgender people, meaning that (in theory) only cisgender people can validate trans folks' gender identity as men or women. For this reason, clients can benefit from exploring what kind of dating and experiences they are after, supporting a healthy relationship with themselves and others and promoting ownership of power and internal validation.

In their own words: dating, relationships and sex

'In their own words' is a collection of interviews of community members carried out by Skye. Here you can read their stories, unadulterated and directly from them. To learn more about the process, review the Preface.

I interviewed Carwyn (they/them) a 25-year-old non-binary person, Charlotte (she/her) a 30-year-old trans woman, and Chrissie (she/her) a 33-year-old trans woman about their experiences of dating, relationships, and sex as trans people. Here are some extracts from our interview together.

The relationship between gender and sexuality

Chrissie: *So it's completely changed everything. Pre-transition, I was very much a straight presenting guy and I had no interest in being with men whatsoever ... Throughout transition, everything was up in the air and now I'm very firmly in the camp of bi and I've now got a boyfriend ... I guess it's the freeing process of transition. It's not just your hormones that change, it's your relationships to yourself and your body.*

Carwyn: *The thing is how many trans friends have said that their sexuality has changed alongside their transition. Obviously, sexuality and gender are different, but there's this interplay of the two that I think a lot of people that I know have experienced.*

Charlotte: *After coming out as trans and transitioning, I was very much more open to exploring the attraction towards men. And I don't think that would've been as easy pre-transition for me ... Dating or a sexual activity with gay men didn't feel right, like I was tricking them in some way.*

Challenges

Anxiety

Chrissie: *When you first come out, you're very uncertain, not very confident. So, to finally put yourself out there in such a vulnerable way, it's a really huge deal. It took me a very long time.*

Safety

Charlotte: *The fear of they're just luring you in to attack or hurt you in any sort of way, be it physically or mentally definitely puts a huge block to dating.*

Chrissie: *I genuinely went to this first date thinking, 'Is this a prank that somebody's playing on me that they're gonna beat me up?' which is pretty grim.*

Carwyn: *I think because I'm quite like 'cis passing', which is a phrase I hate, there is a bit of physical safety in that. Not having ever been on a date and felt unsafe even going.*

Rejection

Charlotte: *The dating sites, nobody reads those things, you try to be clear and either they just stop talking to you or they have a one or two messages after and just trail off.*

Chrissie: *My approach was to be very clear on my profile, turns out nobody really reads those things. They just go off your picture. You could be chatting to someone for a few days and then suddenly they'd be like, 'Do you wanna go for a drink?' Like okay, just to make sure you did see on my profile that I'm trans? And like 99 per cent of the time it's boom, unmatched. Why do I even bother putting it on there?*

Empowerment

Chrissie: *The process of transitioning and coming out involves scary thing after scary thing. I think the one thing I've learned in my life over the last few years is that you've gotta use that fear as a reason to do things and that's why I'm a more confident person now.*

Charlotte: *There's really been two big moments that I felt much more empowered and much happier with my sex life and relationships. After I had my breast augmentation surgery, I just felt more comfortable in myself and it was a huge boost in confidence. And then gender confirmation surgery, things felt right. I had to experiment and find new ways that the new anatomy was pleasured. It was gruelling, but it was also, oh my God, this was amazing. I finally found stuff that I'm happy with. No longer is that dysphoria there and always playing on the back of my mind.*

Carwyn: *For me, certain relationships have been pretty gender affirming. Last year I was dating a trans man and at the same time, I was dating a non-binary person. That was my first experience* *actively dating two people and the combination of polyamory, dating two trans people, and just all of it being really gender affirming and comfortable was really nice.*

Dysphoria

Chrissie: *To begin with I wanted to hide it from my boyfriend, that's not something I would talk about at all towards the beginning. My initial feeling towards the beginning is 'why does he want to be with me in first place when he could just go and be with a cis person?'. I don't wanna scare him off because I'm so very lucky that he's chosen me to be with. He's now done his research so now I can be super open with him if I'm having a really tough day.*

Charlotte: *It made it very difficult when things were coming to get physical with someone. How am I gonna explain to this person something that I don't want them to do without telling them what to do and just dominating the encounter?*

Carwyn: *I was sleeping with my flatmate and they're non-binary and we'd had conversations about dysphoria before we had started sleeping together. They were very respectful with me about it and gave me permission to have boundaries around what we did or didn't do to my body, like explicitly asked me. Having only slept with cis men before, that was one of those light bulb moments of, oh, this is a thing I can do, or I can ask these really specific questions and I can give these really specific answers and boundaries.*

8 | What would God say?

I grew up as a Christian and attended a Catholic school where we prayed once a day and went to mass once a week. My late uncle was a bishop and, perhaps for that reason, my walls were covered in virgins that I collected like Pokémon. My God was split in three, the Holy Spirit (which was agender), father and son, which gave me the impression that the spiritual world too was ruled by the patriarchy. As a woman, I should strive to be gracious, self-sacrificing and pure like the Virgin Mary was. I was told that Jesus loved me and lived inside of me, and although this was somewhat reassuring, as I reached puberty, I was conflicted by having someone monitor my thoughts, as if God had mounted a CCTV system in my brain. I was explicitly instructed to avoid temptation, and to stop myself should I ever feel aroused. I was invertedly told that my body was not mine, desire was sinful and the only way one could enjoy intercourse was in the context of marriage and conception. These messages came from my teachers, my family, the adults I trusted. I look back and, on behalf of my younger self, I feel upset about having had this invisible control imposed over the awakening of my body.

A question for you

Were you raised in any faith or religion?
Is your God or are your deities male, female or agender?
Based on your God's or deities' gender, what kind of assumptions did you form about men, women and non-binary folk?

Religious and spiritual beliefs are often present when working with dysphoria and gender diversity. Traditionally, many religions have condemned anyone who raised a rainbow flag. This means that generations of believers and not-so believers would have been exposed to, and then potentially gone on to internalise, negative messages around gender and sexual diversity. These messages would not only impact transgender and non-binary folk, but also their families and communities, hindering their ability to accept and validate diversity. As a result, and in anticipation of being rejected, many people delay coming out (if they come out at all), or sacrifice undergoing gender-affirming interventions.

Oftentimes when working with LGBTQI+ individuals, we will observe a fundamental conflict between their desire to be close to God and their sense of self, fearing that their faith and identity are irreconcilable. So, how can we support the psychological wellbeing of our clients while being affirming of their gender, sexual and religious identities?

To carry out this part of the work, you ought to forget what you think you know about a specific religion or spiritual belief, focusing on what faith means to the person in front of you. The rules associated with any religion have a variety of interpretations, and what makes someone engage with their faith is personal to them, as it is their degree of engagement. We may be religious because of an inability to challenge what we were taught by the people we love and trust. Some may benefit from a sense of community fortified by songs and rites; these habitual and synchronised behaviours become a crucial part of what make us feel connected to one another, enabling the processing and meaning-making of life's events. Others, above all, strive to be good, and religion delivers a concrete instruction manual on how to achieve this. A few are driven by their fear of death, hell or reincarnating into the wrong kind of creature. Overall, spiritual practices like praying can provide a sense of control, hope and peace. Religious faith broadly acts as a coping strategy that allows us to organise our chaotic and apparently futile existence, while providing some answers for life's complex issues.

Some religions, cults and spiritual groups conceive the body as a sacred gift from God, and a few even believe that humans were made in God's image. Thus, altering one's body could be construed as a sin. This is a common predicament for transgender and non-binary folk, and this belief might stop clients from pursuing a physical transition that could help them alleviate dysphoria. In such instances, you might wonder, are these beliefs enhancing or detrimental to their life? And what is my role as a mental health practitioner? Well, not everyone accepts every element of their religion; certain rites and mandates have a historical basis and conform to tradition rather than to a principle that is core to twenty-first-century living. After all, law, science and society have evolved a fair bit since most sacred scriptures were written. There are Muslims with and without a hijab, and fervent Jews who attend the synagogue once a year. So, to what degree does your client believe and follow any religious principles that they may have?

While sharing your client's religious identity might facilitate a common understanding of the experiences that surround it, hence reducing contextual explanations, not sharing the same religious background can also bring advantages, like looking at its components with fresh eyes and being more prone to enquire about the reasons and symbology behind it, rather than taking these for granted. Whatever your background is, aim to strike a balance between curiosity and self-learning. Consider parallel processes within therapy, and how when working with religious themes, you might be transferentially enacting the figure of the minister. While working with Catholic individuals, within therapeutic disclosures, you might find a replication of dynamics of confession and absolution. Be mindful of power dynamics and of persuading clients to let go of their beliefs. Your duty is to simply be a mirror, allowing them to make a decision that would support their most authentic way of living. Wilcox (2002) and Levy and Lo (2013) researched ways in which LGBT individuals managed to reconcile their queer identities and faith, reporting that they had developed a more individualised faith, rather than rigorously conforming to institutional church doctrine. However, this approach leaves unaddressed the experiences of families of trans and non-binary folk. When coming out to them, the first thought of many parents might be, 'My child is going to hell. I must have done something wrong. I must pray to make it better.' Supporting families to reconcile their faith and gender diversity is a core part of the therapy.

Explorations with clients who are people of faith

- Why do you think you are trans or non-binary (i.e., is this a curse, a product of diversity, God's will)?
- If you had to guess, what does God say about you being trans or non-binary?
- What do you think God expects you to do in relation to your dysphoria?

Pray the gay away, and other conversion therapies

The Netflix documentary *Pray Away* (Stolakis, 2021) follows LGBTQI+ individuals who, at some stage in their lives, joined religious-affiliated conversion therapy programmes. Conversion therapy can be defined as a group of techniques commonly ranging from pseudo-psychological treatments to spiritual counselling, intended to change someone's sexual orientation or gender identity (Government Equalities Office, 2018). Among other events, the 1980s HIV crisis increased the visibility of gender and sexually diverse people and provided [religious-affiliated] conversion therapy groups with leverage to convince the public that their 'life choices' were being punished by God. Suddenly, not only salvation of the soul, but of one's actual life was at stake.

Many queer and trans folk raised in faith systems knew that if they were to name their identity, they would be shunned. With the appearance of reparative praying groups, a route to acceptance arose. In confessing one's torments, one could experience relief and obtain social support, becoming once again part of the group. This presented hope in that – as those with lived experience testified – 'you have a choice; you don't have to be gay or trans'. Many LGBTQI+ people married in a heteronormative fashion, had families and tried not to engage with their identity. The principle was that you are only gay if you are doing 'gay things', or that you are only trans if you are presenting in a gender-affirming manner. Some of the interviewees spoke about how, while immersed in this reality, they found a safe space. Tragically, this space was only safe for one version of themselves, that which was congruent with God's will (whatever that was thought to be). Contrary to what many of us were told, God's love seemed to be conditional and restricted to straight and cis people.

Over the years, I have come across several LGBTQI+ people whose sense of shame in relation to their diversity (i.e., internalised transphobia and/or homophobia) was closely linked to their spiritual beliefs, or those that they were raised with. The National LGBT Survey (Government Equalities Office, 2018) looked at a variety of issues relevant to gender and sexual diverse people: 108,100 individuals participated in this study, 13 per cent were transgender and 6.9 per cent were non-binary. One would think that reparative therapy rarely happens, however they discovered that a total of 5 per cent of all respondents had been offered it. Exclusively looking at the experience of trans and non-binary people, 8 per cent had been offered conversion therapy, and 4 per cent underwent it. So, who is encouraging conversion therapy to 'cure' lesbian, gay, bisexual and transgender people? The same study determined that in 52.2 per cent of cases the suggestion came from faith organisations, 28.5 per cent were encouraged by family members, and in 11.9 per cent of cases it was healthcare professionals. The picture varies from country to country and, in the US, a study looking at the experiences of 27,500 transgender people found that 14 per cent received encouragement to change their identity, and 5 per cent engaged with interventions (Turban et al., 2019).

On being affirming, yet exploratory

In 2022, the UK government introduced a bill which proposes a ban for conversion therapy for sexual orientations in people under the age of 18. This contemptuous piece of legislation not only failed to protect sexually diverse individuals above this age, but it deliberately failed to address conversion therapy practices for gender identity issues. Currently, trans and non-binary folk find themselves vulnerable to this gruesome practice. Something to note is that one of the reasons provided by the government was that gender-diverse people might seek psychological support to address dysphoria, and that including gender diversity in such bill would potentially impact the therapy. As I am writing these lines, hundreds of LGBTQI+ organisations have shown their outrage, but there is not yet a resolution. It seems like, from a governmental perspective and when it comes to gender identity, there are no clear boundaries in ethical psychological practices.

So, is it possible to question your client's desire to transition while being affirming, or would this constitute an attempt to deliver conversion therapy? I believe that it is possible and often even necessary to support a deeper exploration of client's desires to transition, but only if this is brought by the client as a therapeutic question, not as a standard form of operating with all people. Additionally, some might want to address questions like, 'Am I really trans, or do I just like presenting in feminine clothing? Will it be worth transitioning, or will I regret it?' The length of time and intensity of your client's gender feelings can help contextualise their identity and the likely trajectory of their desire to transition. Ultimately, your role as a therapist is to understand your client's apprehensions and wishes, supporting them to make an informed decision. Whatever the choice, there is always sacrifice, a route that was not taken, a version of us that was not realised. Some people struggle with this idea and wish to have all doors open, but eventually all of us end up having to commit to one, even if that one is a decision not to make a decision.

What would God say?

Max arrived slightly late to their appointment; they were flushed and breathless. 'Take a couple of minutes,' I said. And, with refreshed energy, they declared, 'Ready.' At the age of 38, Max was coming to therapy for the first time. They had a supportive wife and daughter, and they were out to everyone. But after years of openly living as a non-binary transmasculine person (assigned female at birth), Max felt stuck in their transition, and unable to decide what to do next. They had been toying with the idea of what their life would be like if they were to have a deeper voice, or if they no longer had a female-looking chest. It was clear to them that the main barrier to moving forward was their fear of what God would say. I started to question what linked them to God and how religion had entered their life.

Max did not come from a religious family, but their father had converted in later life. As Max proceeded to speak about him, a different energy permeated the room. Their eyes glimmered with admiration and they appeared to be younger. Max's father played the drums, rode motorcycles and in his spare time volunteered as a fireman. While standing in front of walls of fire, he faced the insignificance of his own humanity. He lost friends and saw others disfigured by the flames. The accumulated trauma had triggered a deep depression and, in the midst of questioning 'what's the point of all this?', Max's father found meaning in God.

As a child, Max followed him everywhere. Their father saw right through them, recognising that Max enjoyed all things masculine the most, so he treated them like a boy. Even though Max had a younger brother, Max was the apple of their father's eye. This ignited rivalries between the siblings that carried all the way through adulthood. When Max's father died, their life was torn apart. Some months after the funeral, Max came out, but their brother refused to accept their identity, and often with an ominous tone reminded them of the word of God. Now that the siblings were fatherless, they fought for the preservation of his memory and religious legacy. Through following God's will, the siblings ensured that their father would be proud of them and present in their lives.

Though Max felt paralysed, hating their chest and feeling incongruent towards other parts of their body, they were overcome with guilt for their desires to 'mutilate' the temple of God. I could feel their increasing anguish as these words fell out of their mouth. 'Let's slow down', I suggested. To Max, God represented love, this invisible presence that looks down from above. It did not take us long to recognise that when Max was asking, 'What would God say?' they were referring to their father. Max spoke about not having the opportunity to come out to him and, now that he was gone, Max's brother had made himself custodian of their father's voice.

We separated Max's anxieties around what their father would have thought and focused on what we knew about him. In life, Max's father was already accepting of their masculinity and always encouraged them to be happy, so what could we infer in relation to their wish to have surgery and potentially HRT? Max liberated themselves from the weight of the scriptures, and from that point worked on how to keep themselves happy, as well as the memory of their father alive.

Final thoughts

It is not only the duty of gender-diverse people to work through these feelings, but also of those belonging to faith groups. Kennedy (2008) explored Christian ideas on transgender identities and proposed ways for churches to establish a balance between a literal interpretation of the Bible and compassion for gender-diverse people. Similarly, Stone (2007) explored ways in which church members could demonstrate love and tolerance for gender-diverse communities by creating an environment of acceptance. In the UK, there are already LGBTQI+ affirmative temples belonging to a variety of faiths and one can only hope that this is the beginning and that more will arise.

9 Clients' relationship with the mirror

The ruler with which we measure our appearance is capricious and ever-changing. From the plus-size figures of the Italian Renaissance to the cinched-waist of Victorian England, time and culture continuously shape the eyes of the beholder. The social privilege attained by those who we consider to be attractive becomes a target for the rest of us. We have been conditioned to fear fat, wrinkles, asymmetry, the colour of our skin, the texture of our hair, the effect of gravity. So, before you help any of your clients with their own demons, tell me, what do you see when you look in the mirror? Are you at ease with your body? How do these feelings impact your overall confidence, your ability to be naked in front of your partner or to be present while having sex?

Using countless parameters we scrutinise one another, and in one look we might be able to establish a person's socioeconomic status, health, attractiveness or gender conformity. Western ideals portray the perfect man and woman as opposite in their appearance: women should be hairless, curvy and soft and men ought to be muscular, rugged and hairy. However, let's not forget that there are cultural and historical variations in these fads. For instance, in Iran between 1785 and 1925 notions of beauty were largely undifferentiated; the ideal was androgyny and beautiful men and women had similar facial and bodily features (Najmabadi, 2001). Current trends might somewhat originate in biological differences between sexes, but we have also been socialised to further maintain and enhance these traits. In my mind, this carries an underlying message about how, if we look different, perhaps we should also behave differently, have separate roles in society, or even rights. And so, I wonder, what would be the impact of having a non-gendered or androgynous appearance as the norm? Would we focus more on our similarities as opposed to our differences? Would this support the suppression of the tyranny of gender?

Looking after one's image has been advertised as a feminine value, and so we might observe that women actively care for their bodies, whereas men mostly remain masculine by omission. For example, many women regularly shave their body hair and associate not complying with this habit as a sign of being unhygienic or even manly. Hairy armpits have been associated with lesbians, hippies and, to endorse a national stereotype, the French. Women often moisturise their skin and use floral perfumed products, enlarging the gap between a masculine and feminine smell and touch. Some women use tools to attain the very much desired hourglass shape by using padded bras or shapewear. Others look for more permanent measures like breast augmentation surgery, Brazilian butt lifts or cosmetic surgery on their labia. Men on the other hand, to enhance their virility, can access penile enlargement surgery, hair transplants, obsessively hit the gym, grow a beard or even deepen their voice.

Thus, to a degree, most people try to comply with contemporary gendered ideals. Both gender-diverse and cisgender folk might struggle with meeting these canons and with attaining a satisfactory degree of gender congruency. So, ask yourself, how much of my self-image and self-esteem are linked to complying with societal expectations around gender?

First person's perspective: what I feel

How much does your body define you as a person? Your body holds a dual identity; on the one hand, it is an essential and inseparable part of yourself, it is the colour of your eyes, your height, that scar on your cheek. Also, the body is a messenger that communicates information about our surroundings helping us navigate our reality, and thus acting as 'a container, a membrane that both separates and connects our internal world, from the world we live in' (Scarrone Bonhomme, 2019a). When closing your eyes and shutting down the distractions, the noise, the colours, you can enhance non-visual signals, becoming aware of the tightness of those skinny jeans, or the rumbling in your stomach. These sensations are part of what has been defined as the *first-person perspective* (1PP), 'a system of sensory-motor capacities that function without awareness or the necessity of perceptual monitoring' (Gallagher, 2005, p. 24).

Even though trans and non-binary people often speak about their body appearance not matching their internal sense of self, many also describe a general sense of 'wrongness' which is unrelated to looks – a dysregulation in the connectivity to their bodies. Thus, if we were to conceive connectivity as a spectrum, at one end we would find hyper awareness and an overt sense of body presence, in the middle, the ability to tune in and out of specific sensations, and at the other end, a lack of connection. Ataria (2018) suggested that some 'individuals experience the body as being too much their own, they have a sense of overpresence, or in cognitive terms, their sense of body-ownership is too strong' (p.1). I believe this to be particularly prevalent in people who experience gender dysphoria, chronic pain, body dysmorphia or other body and appearance-related struggles.

Gender-diverse folk might often find themselves at extreme ends of this spectrum. For instance, some transmasculine people (assigned female at birth) speak about dysphoria towards their reproductive organs. The knowledge that they have ovaries and a womb, even without the ability to see them or touch them, but only to feel them through period cramps, can trigger a deep sense of incongruence. Thus, 'the visual is not the only means of gender recognition. All our senses need to be considered' (Coleman et al., 2012).

How do we perceive gender incongruence if not exclusively with our eyes? We briefly spoke about *interoception* in the introductory chapter; as you already know, this sense communicates internal bodily signals (e.g. 'my bladder is full', or 'I've broken a bone'). Gender-diverse people might perceive incongruence through interoceptive sensations, for example, a transfeminine person might feel distressed by the pulsating blood flowing towards their genitals that causes an erection or a transmasculine person might experience greater incongruence towards their chest when, due to hormonal changes, it becomes fuller and harder to bind. *Exteroception* relays information from the environment (e.g. 'it is raining', or 'the sun is kissing my skin'). We can perceive gender incongruence through this sense, and commonly transmasculine folk speak about avoiding wearing a bra at the start of puberty, as not only was it a feminine thing to do, but it also increased the awareness towards this body part. In the case of transfeminine people, there might be an affinity towards wearing feminine clothing that not only looked good but felt congruent from a sensory point of view. Lastly, the movement of our bodies in space is communicated through *proprioception* (e.g. 'I am jumping up and down', or 'I am raising my hand'). Gender incongruence is perceived through proprioception in relation to movement and to stereotypical masculine or feminine mannerisms. For instance, some transfeminine people might have been perceived as feminine children, and they might have been bullied for it, eventually learning to repress this part of themselves. Also, some transmasculine people might have been described as tomboys growing up, preferring to behave in a conventionally masculine manner and to engage in rough-and-tumble play. Through the senses of interoception, proprioception and exteroception, gender 'incongruence would therefore manifest when sensing that there is a disconnect; an alienation from one's smell, one's voice, one's touch, generating instinctive feelings of discord and inauthenticity' (Scarrone Bonhomme, 2019a).

The third person perspective: what you see

When we look at our image in a mirror or in a photo, we unintentionally detach from the experience of inhabiting our flesh. We become observers, another person looking inwards. The body shifts into an impersonal and unidimensional object that can be sized and scrutinised. This is described as the *third-person perspective* (3PP). In these instances, the mirror becomes a vehicle that transports us between the 1PP (the body's function and feeling) to the 3PP (the body's image).

When working with individuals who experience gender incongruence, the relationship with the mirror often comes into play, becoming a tool to self-punish, to avoid or to find oneself. If you were to ask your clients how they relate to their image, some might tell you that they use the mirror as a way of discouraging any thoughts of transition. Observing themselves allows them to focus on how they are seen by others, reinforcing thoughts like, 'You will never be a woman, it doesn't matter what you feel.' People who use the mirror as a tool for repression or emotional self-harm are likely to attempt to stay within the 3PP, avoiding connecting with their internal sense of their gender. On the other hand, individuals who wish to remain attuned to their internal sense of self (1PP) might avoid looking in the mirror, as the experience can be confusing and painful. Many people cover mirrors while they shower or avert their gaze when naked. In this way, the mirror can bring vividness or dull gender dissonance. Echoing this idea, (Lin et al., 2014) studied the differences in neural networks of body representation in trans and cisgender individuals, finding that some trans people use coping mechanisms that dissociate bodily emotions from body image.

Some relate to the mirror in helpful ways, facilitating cohesiveness and a better sense of body ownership. This might be, for example, by focusing on features which are congruent to their gender identity, like an agender person might by noticing their genderless body shape. As trans and non-binary folk attain an appearance which is consistent with their identity, their relationship with the mirror is likely to change. Some shift from patterns of avoidance, to overtly seeking to see themselves once they have started hormone replacement therapy, as they might wish to closely monitor change. Individuals who have not yet achieved gender congruency can be encouraged to find a balance between not looking at their image in moments when they are feeling more dysphoric and, when feeling less dysphoric, looking at affirming features or closing their eyes and being present in their bodies. For example, a trans woman who is dysphoric about erections might find mornings particularly triggering (as her levels of testosterone peak at this time). To this you may add that this might be the moment of the day when she spends most time in front of the mirror while she applies make-up. To help clients deal with gender incongruence, you can dedicate a session to understanding your client's routine, experiences of dysphoria, triggers and mechanisms to manage it.

People as walking mirrors

I am torn from myself, and the image in the mirror prepares me for another still more serious alienation, which will be the alienation by others. For others have only an exterior image of me, which is analogous to the one seen in the mirror. Consequently, others will tear me away from my immediate inwardness much more surely than will the mirror.

Merleau-Ponty (1964, p.136).

In encounters when being misgendered, or being looked at as if the other is trying to guess their birth assigned sex, trans and non-binary folk are often brought back to the painful awareness of their gender dissonance, shifting their viewpoint from the 1PP to the 3PP. If indeed people have this power, it might be that we behave towards them just like we do when in front of the mirror. You might want to explore this concept with your client by asking questions like: 'Do you feel like there is a relationship between your ability to look at your reflection in the mirror and your ability to openly relate and look at others?' Or, 'What do you imagine others see when they look at you?' Be mindful that the worry and tension associated with how one may be perceived can act as a self-fulfilling prophecy. Exploring this concept, as well as the one of projection, can help our clients shape and control their reality.

Therapists as mirrors

As the Groupon bottomless brunch with prosecco gets cashed, gangs of girl-friends congregate around the table. Within seconds of that initial hug, you'll hear, 'Babes, I love your dress. You're looking fab. Have you lost weight?' As a woman, I too have been pre-programmed to notice expressions of femininity and to use these cues to connect with my female peers. If someone has made the effort, it seems our responsibility to notice, and to praise the time invested in complying with what society has dictated to be beautiful.

It is not uncommon for clients to use the psychotherapeutic space as a test-ing lab, after all, the gender work is full of first times: first time your client might have accepted to themselves and to you that they are trans, the first time they experienced the effects of oestrogen in their body and, quite frequently, the first time they presented as their true selves in front of someone else. So, when working with trans women or non-binary transfeminine people I have occasionally felt a gravitational pull to replicate this custom. I know that many of my clients had the mirror as their only witness, and when they take the step of sharing their feminine side with me, it is like I owe them some form of recog-nition. However, exchanging affirmations in therapy is a dangerous game and, like self-disclosure, should only be used after careful consideration.

By responding to the client's question, 'Do I look fine to you?' we are affirm-ing the principle that, to exist in this society, clients must present in ways that are acceptable to others, and that their image should be the primary guide to their transition, as opposed to how they feel. This question conceals an under-lying agenda addressing issues like: 'Do I look feminine enough?' 'Do I look beautiful?' 'Can you tell that I am trans by looking at me?' 'Do you accept me as a woman?' The natural desire of every practitioner is to make their client feel good, but impulsively replying is (as my supervisor often reminds me) a wasted opportunity. In responding, we could reinforce power imbalances, by which the therapist is seen as the answer to the client's every question, as well as their source of reassurance.

It can be helpful to explore the origin of these insecurities since many of our clients might have been bullied, frequently because of their gender, sexuality or even neurodiversity being noticed. Others, while hiding, might have been found out presenting in a gender-affirming role in private and might have been shamed for it. These experiences can foster beliefs about one's sense of inade-quacy, and many people are afraid to their core of looking ridiculous or being laughed at. But who are we to say what looks good or feminine enough? What do we really know? Who named us the gender police?

The spotlight effect and social dysphoria

The spotlight effect or egocentric bias (Gilovich et al., 2000) describes how by nature we tend to overestimate the extent of which our appearance and actions are being noticed by others. In one study, university students were asked to wear a flattering or potentially embarrassing t-shirt and to estimate the number of observers who were able to recall the image shown in the t-shirt. Participants estimated that 50 per cent of the other students would have noticed their t-shirt when, in fact, only 25 per cent of the classmates remembered seeing it.

Trans and non-binary people can be hyperaware of their appearance, and of how they are being perceived by others. However, like the rest of us, they are also likely to overestimate the extent to which they are being noticed, and how much others care about them being trans. For more information on this, review Chapter 10 *What if they 'clock' me?*.

What can we do?

So, what do you do when you cannot beat that painful gut feeling that proclaims, 'My body is not mine. It looks and feels wrong,'? Well, you start to avoid, to look around but not directly at, to cover mirrors, to take the pictures rather than being in them. You become an ethereal being, unanchored in space, a floating head. Then, therapy is the place where you dare to relate and look directly at the painful parts of yourself. In my experience, much of internalised transphobia can be dealt with by challenging stigma, learning about queer theory and applying compassion-focused principles; you can review some psychotherapeutic strategies further in Chapter 2 *Working with identity-based trauma*. On the other hand, much of gender dysphoria can be mitigated by body-focused approaches and acceptance commitment therapy. Here are some practical exercises.

After spending some time with your eyes closed appreciating the sensations of your body, write a gratitude letter. For a moment try and forget about how your body looks or what others see when they look at it. Focus on what your body does for you, on how it allows you to perceive the world, to experience pleasure, how it keeps you alive. Allow yourself to connect to it, and to appreciate it and yourself for it.

Standing in front of the mirror, alternate between closing your eyes and connecting to your internal sense of your gender (your masculinity, femininity or neutrality) and gazing at your reflection. Pause and acknowledge any puzzlement caused by gender incongruence, by the split between 1PP and 3PP and, while breathing, sit with it. Try to be fair with your thoughts and to be descriptive rather than judgemental. Create your own statements, such as: 'I feel male inside, and when I look in the mirror, I wish my body would reflect this'; 'It is normal to be trans and to feel this way'; 'It is difficult, but my body is still changing and one day it will match my internal sense of self'.

Use these self-affirmations at the start of the day. We do not walk around telling people how small their hands are, or how masculine their faces are, so why would we do this to ourselves? When you look in the mirror, find yourself and see yourself for more than just a few physical features.

10 What if they 'clock' me?

Walking down the high street, sitting in a busy train carriage or entering a room full of people, some wonder, 'Will I be judged?' Gender-diverse people often talk about a fear of visibility, a wish to make themselves small and imperceptible. It doesn't matter if your identity is binary or non-binary, or how apparent it is to others that you are trans. It doesn't even matter if you are wearing a quintessentially gendered piece of clothing like a cocktail dress or if you are solely using transparent nail polish. The fear of this difference being revealed frequently haunts individuals belonging to these communities, and to be found out to be gender-diverse is sometimes colloquially referred to as 'being clocked'.

So, why might gender-diverse people wish for their identity to remain unnoticed? Well, there are many different reasons, and it is worth exploring them on a case-by-case basis. Commonly, trans folk want to simply be seen as people, not having this label attached to their every action. They might feel burdened by embodying stereotypes or representing the entirety of trans communities. Many want to go about their lives in peace, not having their past examined, and what cis person wouldn't want this for themselves too? Others are conscious of their bodies and experience dysphoria associated with being too masculine or too feminine. So, when being clocked, they might perceive this as a confirmation that they have retained excessive elements associated with their birth-assigned sex, which may be interpreted by them as some kind of failure. Needless to say, being clocked can lead to verbal and physical abuse and, for these and other reasons, some might strive to 'pass' as a cisgender person. However, there is a crucial difference, as it is not the same as the wish not to be seen, rather it is more about being seen as someone who one is not.

Let's talk about 'passing'

Historically, the concept of passing was associated with race and religion, referring to non-white people whose racial identity was not immediately obvious (Haney-López, 1996; López, 2005; Wollrad, 2005). Also, the term was applied to those who were other than Christian, such as Jewish people, who were able to attain the privilege of not being identified as such in Nazi Germany and in the US (Pulver, 1999). Passing originates in social inequalities and power imbalances, in the post-colonial ideology of superiority of the white, the Christian, the cisgender and the straight. 'Notions of passing tend to be predicated upon assumptions of essentialized and naturalized group difference' (Pfeffer, 2014). This argument has been commonly used to refute trans people's rights to claim their gender identity, as seemingly only those born in a male sexed body can identify as men. The same principle applies to females and, well, non-binary identities are just disregarded.

On occasions, passing has been portrayed as an intended deception. Billard (2019) describes how the media has exploited narratives of transgender people as deceivers who attempt to seduce cisgender heterosexuals. Either way, it seems like there is no way to win: those who 'successfully pass' might be portrayed as malicious and those who do not, as less than. This hierarchical split is policed by both cis and trans people. Those belonging to 'superior groups' (in this case, cisgender people) might worry about their privilege being taken away, this being the main argument used by socio-political groups like trans-exclusionary radical feminists (TERFs) who argue that equality rights for trans women will be detrimental to those already attained by cis women. On the other hand, gender-diverse people might be particularly critical of those who aren't able to attain these standards of appearance, potentially becoming bad representatives of the communities. This is to say, the perception is that those who do not pass will end up drawing more attention towards themselves and by extension, their communities, bringing further shame to their already stigmatised group.

Gender-diverse people are exposed to these forces regardless of whether the person is interested in conforming to those ideals (Gagné & Tewksbury, 1998), as they are positively reinforced by comments like, 'Oh my, I would have never guessed that you were trans,' or negatively reinforced by remarks like, 'Look at her hands, she will never pass.' What we must not forget is that for most, their visibility is not a choice, but the result of biology and/or not having sufficient economic means to afford the interventions that would allow them to achieve congruency, and (if wishing so) to reduce visibility. In the words of Sánchez & Schlossberg (2001), 'like queer identity itself, passing can be experienced as a source of radical pleasure or intense danger; it can function as a badge of shame or a source of pride' (p.3).

On conformity

Traditions are harder to shake off than we might think. They provide us with a sense of rhythm and safety, and as we repeatedly perform them, we become increasingly invested in them. Therefore, as time passes, we are less likely to scrutinise their relevance. For example, within the dominant Western culture, traditional ideas around masculinity and femininity have shaped generations, pushing men towards repressing their emotions, avoiding femininity, placing importance on sex (rather than romance) and expressing themselves in the square shapes of toughness and dominance (McDermott et al., 2019). Traditional ideas around femininity have domesticated and tamed women, painting them as irrational and emotional. They have emphasised their modesty, fidelity and care for children but, above all, they have placed importance on their appearance (Mahalik et al., 2005). These ideas have pushed men and women towards opposite ends of an imaginary spectrum, having shoehorned our ability to express ourselves freely and authentically.

It should not come as a surprise to anyone that the influence of these standards is not restricted to cisgender people, but that trans and non-binary folk are also shaped by them, although research indicates that it might be to a lesser degree. A recent study carried out by McDermott et al. (2021) found that (in a decreasing order of influence) cisgender men, cisgender women and lastly gender-diverse folk showed signs of conformity to traditional gendered values. This conformity was manifested in their appearance, behaviour and attitudes. So, the issue for trans folk would not be limited to 'Do you pass from a visual point of view?' but, also encompass 'Do you conform to how women or men are expected to be, think, feel and behave?'.

Masculine, feminine and non-binary visibility

There are a number of factors that will play a part in how visible a person's trans identity is, and thus how likely they are to be clocked. Among them you might think about how old the person was when they commenced hormone replacement therapy (since the earlier they transition, the less likely they are to retain features associated to their sex), how many gender-affirming interventions have they accessed, what choices they make in terms of their gender presentation, but also where they live, as gender-diverse people living in larger towns or in LGBTQI+ friendly cities might enjoy greater invisibility than those living in very normative, traditional and smaller areas. Not limited to this, transmasculine, transfeminine and non-binary people face different challenges in relation to their visibility.

Interestingly, it is easier to masculinise a body than it is to feminise it. Masculinising hormone therapy allows for changes in muscle mass, deepening of the voice and increased body and facial hair growth. So, if a person chose to surgically remove their breasts, there would not be many external visual indicators that a person was assigned female at birth. Some trans men and (non-binary) transmasculine people experience dysphoria towards their height, or having smaller than average hands or feet when compared to a typical cis man. However, these do not tend to draw as much attention from the public. For transmasculine people, and as they tend to enjoy greater invisibility than transfeminine people, the challenge is different. I commonly meet trans men who, years after having transitioned (and particularly if they're stealth), might continue to worry about being 'discovered'. Some may go to great lengths to avoid the conversation leading to this disclosure and might place themselves at an arm's length from their circle of friends, concerned that if they are to come out (just like before having transitioned) they could be rejected.

Trans women and (non-binary) transfeminine people are more frequently 'clocked', as hormone therapy does not alter bone structure or voice. Often, individuals may be read as trans due to having retained one or many of these features: square jaw line, brow line, Adam's apple, shoulder width, height, size of hands or feet, or receding hairline. These features might not only cause dysphoria, but also make them more visible to others, and more likely to experience both transphobia and misogyny (Serano, 2007). In my clinical experience, in comparison to transmasculine people, transfeminine people can develop a greater tolerance to being looked at and clocked. This might become part of their day-to-day and so through repeated exposure, they might come to accept their visibility. However, they can also worry more often about their safety.

It is challenging to talk broadly about non-binary people as they may present in a traditional masculine or feminine role, as well as in an androgynous or undetermined manner. For those whose identity includes elements which, to others, might not sit neatly in either category, they are likely to be confronted with looks and assumptions. Some non-binary people may enjoy challenging people's preconceptions around gender, whereas others might compromise to present in a more traditionally binary manner to avoid being singled out.

To you, what does it mean to be clocked?

The psychological dynamics of passing are connected to custom-made roots situated not only in our society and history, but also in the individual's lived experience. To exemplify this, we will unearth Olivia's and Luca's own relationship with being clocked.

I called out her name and she quickly emerged from the waiting room, she kept her sunglasses on and, leading the way to my office, she seemed to minutely examine every tile on the floor. 'Thank you,' she said with a soft-spoken voice. I could sense her heart beating like a hummingbird's. She gently smiled but could not make her eyes meet mine. I was intrigued. Olivia was only young; at 19 she had a life already packed with difficulties. She grew up having a strong sense of self, but her father's stares gradually tamed her, forcing her to develop a diametrically opposite sense of shame. Olivia's parents had a turbulent relationship, shouting and arguing, and the tang of rum constantly infused the air. They held cyclical patterns of honeymoon periods, followed by war, and then quiet departures. Unexpectedly, one day her father didn't come back, finally allowing her to wonder whether, away from his gaze, she could finally be herself. But Olivia's mum had already taken a radical decision to turn their lives around in joining what she hoped to be a stable community for her and her child. The Jehovah's Witness community represented the opportunity to apparently do the right thing, and she grabbed it with both hands. To start with, Olivia enjoyed it, as there were plenty of children to play with, but whatever joy she extracted, it soon evaporated as she became more comfortable and started to show her feminine self. Olivia's love for dancing and dressing up were promptly noticed by the elders: 'Your child is confused, and he must be rectified!' Mum understood that who her 'son' was could not be rectified. Perhaps it wasn't in God's plans to save 'him', so, with an uncertain degree of pain, Olivia was sent away to live with extended family. Shortly after, they too found her to be a nuisance and, in an unfortunate chain of events, she ended up touring foster homes across Britain. Logically, she accepted that if anyone was to notice that she was trans, they would stare and, like many before them, she would be met with an invitation to find the nearest exit.

Olivia's trans identity seems, to me, to be comparable to that of a refugee. Grant et al. (2011) and Begun and Kattari (2016) have similarly found that gender-diverse people are twice as likely to experience homelessness as other members of the general population. Also, Begun and Kattari (2016) explained that individuals whose trans identity is more visible are more likely to become homeless, as well as to face more negative experiences while living in shelters. This even extends to healthcare settings, where the more frequently that a gender-diverse person can pass as cisgender, the lower their likelihood is of experiencing discrimination (Kattari et al., 2015).

So, how are Olivia's worries different to someone's who strives to pass as cisgender? Meet Luca, a second-generation Italian living in London; always impeccably dressed and partial to a good party. Like a nuclear power station, Luca alone can light up a room. Luca transitioned in his twenties and even though he just passed 50, he often jokes and warns me about the terrifying effects of 'old age'. It took us a year of therapy before he was able to say the word 'transgender'. If nowadays you are to ask him about his identity, he might come to say that he was born female. A lot of the initial stages of therapy felt like decoding sessions. As it happens, speaking in riddles can be quite a talent, and Luca was not explicit about anything to do with his body, his identity or his history. Out of sight, out of mind. To reconcile him with the negative stereotypes he had faced around trans people (and by extension himself), he reluctantly joined a trans support group, but he could not see himself as part of the community. His burden was to be carried alone.

At one session Luca was unusually quiet. Generally he didn't require much prompting, so I was suspicious of his silence. Luca told me he was embarrassed about what he had done. 'What is wrong with me?' he said. 'What kind of person does that?' The week leading to the appointment, Luca had gone for a check-up to his GP. He sat in the waiting area, staring at the screen displaying patients' names and room numbers, and as he was being entertained by his thoughts, a woman approached him. 'Is Vittoria your sister?' she said. 'I went to school with her.' 'You see,' Luca said to me, 'I also went to Vittoria's school and so this would mean that she would know who I was. I had no option. I denied it. It was ridiculous because an instant later the screen displayed both my name and surname and so, it must have been clear to her, but I just couldn't!' Luca did not hide behind sunglasses, but promised himself never to use social media; he'd avoid greeting the friend of the friend of his third cousin. He lives in an area where he is likely to be recognised, yet that would be the worst of his nightmares. He is full of contradictions – those of someone who both hides and apparently subconsciously wants to be found out.

As you can see, people may choose to conceal their trans identity for many different, individual reasons, although shame tends to be at the core of them. And different gender identities are posed with different challenges around passing and being clocked.

Exploring concerns around being clocked

As previously mentioned in the section *Let's talk about passing*, this concept can refer not only to gender-diversity, but to someone's race, religion, ethnicity, sexuality and other intersectional parts of their identity which might bring shame or discrimination to their life. So, initially, you might try and identify who the person is as a whole and what strategies they use to mask their difference. For example, if your client is both gender-diverse and neurodiverse, you might consider with them the parallels between masking their autism and concealing their trans identity.

More specifically, focusing on fears around being clocked as trans define to what degree your client may be concerned. For example, on a scale from 1 to 10, 1 being 'I do not mind if someone realises that I am trans', 10 being 'I am terrified that someone would notice', where does your client place themselves? Also, are they challenging these fears by exposure and carrying on with their life? Or do they feel constrained by their fear of going out, or forming relationships? Do they feel more threatened by members of the public realising their identity, or is it more about the people in their lives who are currently unaware?

There tends to be a correlation between features associated with a person's birth-assigned sex and those which would be noticed by others as giveaways of someone's trans identity. It is difficult to discern how much of someone's discomfort is caused by incongruence towards a body part and how much of it is linked to a fear of rejection, or a lack of integration with the broader world. In most cases, it would be rather difficult to draw a clear-cut line but it is worth posing this question to the client to reflect on their motivation for concealment.

Make-up tends to be an effective tool of concealment, and transfeminine people, in particular, might get caught in lengthy processes of applying layers of protection, reinforcing the fallacy that without it they cannot be seen in front of others. This is not exclusive to trans women, of course, since many cisgender women have also been indoctrinated into thinking that a mask of makeup is needed in order for them to be socially acceptable.

What do you do when you do not want to be noticed? Looking down, wearing hats, sunglasses, earplugs, headphones or pretending that the world is not there. These strategies are used not only by those who experience dysphoria, but by those who are fearful of rejection. Therefore, clients who are both gender-diverse and neurodiverse might be particularly prone to coping in this way. When we fear being seen, we might have underlyingly concerns about becoming passive and petrified, as if the observer held the powers of the mythological Greek creature Medusa. We forget that we too can bring a response into action, stealing some of that power back, becoming both the observed and the observer. Realistically, we do not know the reason why someone might be looking at us. They might think that we are attractive, we might remind them of someone else, or they might indeed be wondering, 'Is this person trans?' If this was the case, one should not despair; after all, being trans is a minority group. For this reason, your client might be the first ever trans person that the passer-by has seen. Evidently, it is not polite to stare, but rather than assuming that the person is disgusted, or has intentions of harming them, perhaps we could work towards assuming that they are curious and potentially harmless. When confronted with a neutral situation, explore what assumptions are made and what they might say about your client's inner life.

What feelings might your client be avoiding? Olivia avoided being cast out and Luca avoided facing his identity (if others don't know, then I too can forget my identity). Based on your client's experience, what is it that they avoid? Is it feeling ugly, like a joke, embarrassed or disgusting? Does this link to concerns around being verbally or physically attacked? And are these concerns embedded in a history of bullying at school, in a close friend's experience of assault or simply from anxiety driven by following news reports? Some people might not be out to everyone in their life, or even at work, and might fear losing their job. Understand your client's hesitance to let go of this hypervigilance and that, depending on their history or environment, this survival skill may be almost impossible to let go of.

It is important that you too examine your own reactions. If your client is presenting in their gender-affirming role with you, what were your initial impressions of their appearance? If you were to see them on public transport, what would your reaction have been? If you have seen someone who is trans in public before, have you experienced curiosity and perhaps looked for a bit longer than is acceptable?

To conclude, some trans people wish that they had been born in the body matching their identity (i.e., to be a cisgender man or woman). They might feel like their lives would have been easier if they had. But, whatever the case, it is an impossibility and, in my view, mulling over this magical option can only induce further pain, shame and denial of who one is. It is the person's choice to live openly or in 'stealth', and our role as therapist is to support a space where they can weigh up the pros and cons of each option, gradually developing greater acceptance of their identity and reality. We should aim at striking a balance between meeting the person's individual needs to reduce their dysphoria, alongside challenging taken-for-granted societal ideas around beauty and the superiority of cisgender identities.

11 Digital tools and online identities

Contextualising the change

Up until recently, if you were to ask anyone, 'What do you imagine when I say therapy?' some might have mentioned a small room with dimmed lights, a suggestive box of tissues, a glass of water to help drown awkward silences, the therapist's penetrating eyes deciphering their subject, a notebook that keeps secrets, the nodding 'mmmm', the 'What do you think it means?' and the ever-present 'Shall we unpack this?'

Times have changed tremendously since Freud asked the Wolf Man to lay down on his couch. Not only do we work with the unconscious but now we are able to map the neural networks where it resides. We have developed protocols in the shape of endless acronyms, CBT, ACT, CFT, EMDR, that rebrand our understanding of the whys and hows. We have developed medicines and are finally en route to unveiling the under-explored world of psychedelic therapy. But all this has taken close to 150 years. In 2020 we witnessed the most powerful and fast-paced change of our profession, as the outbreak of COVID-19 forced us and our clients to re-evaluate what makes therapy work. When it was no longer safe or desirable to share the same air, we were herded into working within digital and remote spaces.

Like countless others, within a couple of weeks I went from having a full set of in-person clients to reshaping my ways, my setting, my tools and my boundaries to adapt to remote therapy. I was left hanging with a thousand questions that not only belonged to me, but also to my supervisors and supervisees as together we learned to navigate emotions from a distance. The main question was: 'Will it work?' Well, videoconferencing appears to be as effective as in-person care (Hilty et al., 2013). Promisingly, Kocsis and Yellowlees (2018) found that remote therapy offered novel ways to reach and form strong psychotherapeutic relationships with a broad variety of clients, fostering therapeutic intimacy in ways that in-person psychotherapy cannot. It was around that time that I became head of the (remote) mental health service at Teladoc Health UK & Ireland, a service that focused on exclusively providing telephone therapy. In the early days of the pandemic, my team and I learned as we went. Many of us had never delivered full courses of therapy over the phone before then, and some were sceptical about its potential. But two years after its commencement, and with research to back us up, we have become convinced of its disarming power.

The pandemic forced us to stop, to spend long periods of time at home with ourselves, flatmates, partners or family. This social isolation was a blessing for some and a curse for others. In the aftermath of lockdowns, I can see how this was a period of reflexivity where some gender-diverse people, deprived of avoidant strategies to cope with their questioning and dysphoria, came to terms with their identity. Over the course of these couple of years, some were relieved from social anxiety and fears of being clocked, others enjoyed using the mask as it protected them from being visible, and a few found themselves to be in danger as they were trapped in the same household with transphobic partners and families. Moreover, the healthcare crisis brought on by the pandemic particularly impacted trans communities, elongating the already long waiting times to access gender specialist care.

Despite the crisis, there are positives to be found, such as the increased access to mental health support with the popularisation of remote and digital therapy. This has been particularly important for gender-diverse people, as they can often struggle to find a gender-informed therapist in their local area. Testament to this, I can say that my clients are located everywhere in the UK, and some even abroad. Although it is not only about accessibility to a practitioner, but also about preserving safety for individuals who might be at risk if going out as themselves. As explored in Chapter 10 *What if they 'clock' me?* this can be particularly the case for trans women and non-binary folk. Further, the National LGBT survey in the UK reported that trans women were less likely to have accessed mental health services compared to trans men and non-binary respondents (Government Equalities Office, 2018).

On telephone therapy

Dialogue in the Dark was an immersive sensory exhibition run in East London. This rather unusual event was set in total darkness allowing attendees to gaze (for the lack of a better word) into the day-to-day life of visually impaired people. Once in the venue, we locked away our belongings and any object that shed light as, for the next few hours, we were about to relinquish sight. Lined up in a small room, and guided by a visually impaired person, we waited for the 'go' signal to be released into a pitch-black world. There, recreated, was a park, a bus, a market and even a café. Not blinded by vision, my senses relayed smells, textures and noises, as I started to invent colours and shapes to accompany these sensations. I repeatedly bumped into others who were as lost as I was, physical boundaries melted and, without having been introduced, we held and guided one another through space. I sat on what my hands recognised to be a wooden bench, and someone sat close to me. I felt her shoulder pressing against mine and we spontaneously started to talk. I cannot recall the content of the conversation, but I do recall the intimacy and freedom I experienced, not being led by her facial expressions to navigate my words, not having to police myself with socially acceptable smiles, or nodding to show my understanding. We just co-existed and interacted in this invisible space.

Telephone therapy is an under-explored medium of work that can replicate some of these qualities. Like many therapists when first using this medium, I feared losing my visual compass, but seeing can be a deceitful tool. Smiles can cover the sadness in someone's voice, as clients attempt to protect us from peering behind their mask, from uncovering the expressions of the acceptable child, the false self. As professionals in a position of power, our clients might look to us and hint at a desire to be praised. A client once asked me, 'Laura, do you think I look fine?' I paused and questioned her back, 'Why you ask?' For a few sessions now, she had become increasingly worried about my lack of comments on her appearance. She may have been projecting her own fears, taking this as a clear sign that she did not look feminine enough to be praised. When working with clients who display insecurities around their bodies or overall image (like in the case of gender dysphoria or body dysmorphia), there is a risk that clients might frequently ask for reassurance. Like a sugar rush, this reassurance is short lived, leaving the person with withdrawal symptoms. While trans people explore their gender expression, they might be left feeling vulnerable and slightly unsure of themselves; this is when they should be encouraged to grow their self-reliance and internal locus of control. In these cases, the use of telephone therapy removes expectations of validation around their gender performance.

Gender-affirming telephone therapy

You can opt to use telephone-delivered sessions when exploring the client's internal sense of gender, helping them focus on their bodily sensations, as opposed to their appearance.

Clients who might not yet be ready to engage in the session while presenting in an affirming manner might benefit by telephone sessions. These can be used to explore their concerns about how they might be perceived should we see them in that moment.

Working digitally

No medium of communication is perfect and, like any other, videoconference has its pros and cons. It is thought that, compared to in-person therapy, videoconference has the potential to increase empathy in both practitioner and client, as in our screens we have a closer look at the person's micro-expressions, those which would be harder to appreciate if sitting at a distance from each other. It is undeniable that when only seeing head and shoulders we might be prone to overtly focus on the content of the conversation, omitting bodily manifestations of emotions. However, we can overcome this by asking clients to be our eyes where we cannot see, by self-observing their reactions and relaying these to us (e.g., 'Since we started talking about the possibility of using female changing rooms at the gym, I started to fidget').

Working with gender-diverse people, or indeed with anyone who might struggle with their appearance, there are considerations we should account for.

The first consideration is that videoconference programmes such as Zoom, FaceTime or Skype are likely to display both of your faces while you speak. This is something that does not happen during in-person therapy, thus in a digital environment we might be more restricted and guided by our own image and expressions. I have certainly noticed a tendency to monitor myself while in sessions, which at times has been distracting, and at others has provided useful feedback as to how well or indeed, badly, I am conveying the compassion or neutrality I intended. Similarly, clients might restrict their own reactions, hiding their true emotions behind a mask. In these situations, we can use this medium as a tool, asking clients to look at their expressions as they speak to ascertain the veracity, connection or disconnection they experience (e.g., 'When you mentioned that you no longer speak with your father because he rejected you when you came out to him, you seemed somewhat disconnected. I would like you to repeat what happened in a few sentences while you observe yourself, and then tell me what emotions it evokes in you').

Some might be averse towards looking at themselves, whereas others might be unable to observe themselves, perhaps even not paying as much attention to what is going on in the session. You might find the latter in individuals who wish to have great control over their image and appearance. When appropriate, you can agree with the client to use the 'hide' settings to not see themselves. Individuals who struggle with dysphoria in relation to their face might find themselves particularly triggered by their image being shown on screen. We can therefore use the camera as a tool to increase tolerance. As described in Chapter 9, *Clients' relationship with the mirror*, we can encourage clients to focus on their internal feelings, as opposed to what they look like. As we would during in-person sessions, we can use the camera as a mirror, asking the client to look at themselves and to narrate what gets triggered in them, exploring what kind of self-relational patterns they have formed, for example, are they irritated by their image? Do they struggle with perfectionism and worry that they do not apply their makeup well enough?

The digital world

Online forums

Digital spaces play an important role for minority and stigmatised communities, facilitating a number of functions and removing some of the obstacles of the offline world. Working with trans and non-binary people of all ages, I have repeatedly heard how they came across a post or a vlog that opened their eyes to the existence of gender diversity and to the possibilities of transition. In this way, online forums are crucial to the dissemination of information and normalisation of the existence of trans folk. This is especially relevant for people who reside in small and traditional towns, or countries where being gender-diverse might be penalised by law.

Learning about diversity is only the first step, and some people relay how, not yet having come to terms with their identity, their curiosity kept drawing them into reading Reddit posts with headings like 'Am I cis and confused or is this denial?' or 'What are the signs that you are in trans denial?'. Online communication is characterised by a high level of self-disclosure (Boase, 2006; Faccio et al., 2013; Greene et al., n.d.) and, as mentioned with telephone therapy, there is a reduction of concerns around the reaction of people who we cannot see. Some gender-questioning people might not be ready to open up to people in their life and may feel more secure within online confidentiality, expressing their emotions without having to carry them all the way through to transition.

Once decided that accessing interventions or gender specialist support is the way forward, many use these spaces to provide and receive practical help around the potential of interventions. Tumblr, YouTube and TikTok are often used to document the impact of hormones or surgery. Also, there is a great amount of bureaucracy that comes with being trans, and online forums hold an archive of instructions of how to navigate the system. Lastly, as we explored in Chapter 8, *What would God say?*, many trans and non-binary folk are rightfully concerned about the type of support or the lack thereof they might receive when speaking with a healthcare professional. And these forums can often help to report on what the experience has been like when speaking with this or that specialist.

Some clients have also spoken about how social media has provided them with a platform to come out to others in their life, receiving positive responses and allowing them to later go into the physical world more confidently.

Anchoring gender-diverse identity in the world

The inner workings of social media are starting to be common knowledge. Documentaries like *The Instagram Effect* (Jenkin, 2022) or *The Social Dilemma* (Orlowski-Yang, 2020) describe the power they hold over our self-image and world view and how algorithms work to create these addictive spaces. However, clients may or may not know that these algorithms identify the kind of content they pay most attention to, to feed them similar information. As when shopping online and receiving a notification of 'You might also like this', machine learning can use a number of data points, such as where do your eyes look, or how long you spend reading a post. The problem is that this creates echo chambers, designing a tailored-made homogenous display of information, which is not representative of the real world. Many people report how following certain influencers convinced them that they ought to lose weight, get fillers or travel more. The trap has not only been set for those who follow but also for those who post, as they become dependent on social approval.

What is the potential impact of these platforms on trans and non-binary communities? There is a clear exposure to beauty canons and expectations of what transition can achieve. Many of these posts are created by younger people who have had less time to masculinise or feminise (in line with their birth-assigned sex); this repeated exposure to their content could promote 'passing ideals' or those of perfectionism. Some of my clients have told me that having these constant images of 'successful and attractive' trans people can be a drip of hope, reminding them that one day they too can transition, whereas others describe them as a source of pain in such comments as, 'What is the point in transitioning if I am never going to look as "convincing" as this influencer?'

Additionally, there is a risk to using social media as a source of information. For example, if I am interested in learning about hate crime towards LGBTQI+ communities or TERF narratives, even when my curiosity is satisfied, the algorithm will systematically and repeatedly continue to feed me information matching this criterion. This repeated exposure to hate crime might give me the impression that it is a lot more common than one might think, and even elicit fears that I am not safe. These algorithms are not designed to provide you with an accurate image of the world, but to hook your attention with content that will keep your eyes on the screen.

Lastly, even though many might feel protected from the world in the comfort of their own homes, the internet is not free from expressions of transphobia. Public forums can further consolidate ideas around the value of passing, having a normative body or invalidating the experiences of some members of the community – often, those belonging to its subsections like non-binary people. On the other hand, the same spaces can also facilitate political and social activism (Shapiro, 2004).

Explorations around social media use

- What sort of content do you follow in social media?
- How is this content making you feel about your trans identity?
- What would happen if you stopped using social media, posting or stopped following certain content?

Digital self-portrayal

As a brief mention, there is a large proportion of trans and non-binary folk who also belong to the gaming communities. In sessions, clients have mentioned how online gaming has allowed them to escape from their bodies, immersing themselves into alternative realities. Some clients have used their avatars as the first ground for exploration of their femininity or masculinity, being able to design specific bodily features, presenting styles and even to use voice modulators while streaming. Gaming can therefore facilitate clients in exploring their gender without consequences. However, when the amount of time spent gaming becomes disproportionate and starts to take over the person's whole life this can negatively impact their wellbeing. Some people might be tremendously fearful of expressing their gender in the offline world or be discouraged by the impossibility of presenting as perfectly as their avatar; in this way, some may become entrapped in an unrealistic digital world.

Therefore, we should aim at supporting our clients to make a positive use of online spaces, where these avatars, forums and profiles are means of gender explorations and expression, and not avoidance of their identities and bodies.

References

Adams, J. L., Jaques, J. D., & May, K. M. (2004). Counseling gay and lesbian families: Theoretical considerations. *The Family Journal, 12*(1), 40–42. doi.org/10.1177/106648 0703258693

Albert Kennedy Trust (2018). *Economic and personal impact of homelessness for LGBTQ young people.* www.akt.org.uk/news/world-homeless-day-2018

Amadio, D. M. (2006). Internalized heterosexism, alcohol use, and alcohol-related problems among lesbians and gay men. *Addictive Behaviors, 31*(7), 1153–1162. doi.org/10.1016/j.addbeh.2005.08.013

American Psychiatric Association (2000). *Diagnostic and statistical manual of mental disorders: DSM-IV-TR.* scholar.google.com/scholar?cluster=14986546397044054780& hl=en&as_sdt=2005&sciodt=0,5

American Psychiatric Association (2013). *Diagnostic and statistical manual of mental disorders* (5th ed.). Arlington, VA: American Psychiatric Publishing.

Applegarth, G., & Nuttall, J. (2016). The lived experience of transgender people of talking therapies. *International Journal of Transgenderism, 17*(2), 66–72. doi.org/10.1080 /15532739.2016.1149540

Aramburu Alegría, C. (2013). Relational and sexual fluidity in females partnered with male-to-female transsexual persons. *Journal of Psychiatric and Mental Health Nursing, 20*(2), 142–149. doi.org/10.1111/J.1365-2850.2011.01863.X

Arcelus, J., Claes, L., Witcomb, G. L., Marshall, E., & Bouman, W. P. (2016). Risk factors for non-suicidal self-injury among trans youth. *The Journal of Sexual Medicine, 13*(3), 402–412. doi.org/10.1016/j.jsxm.2016.01.003

Ataria, Y. (2018). *Body Disownership in Complex Posttraumatic Stress Disorder.* New York: Palgrave Macmillan. doi.org/10.1057/978-1-349-95366-0

Auyeung, B., Baron-Cohen, S., Ashwin, E., Knickmeyer, R., Taylor, K., & Hackett, G. (2009). Fetal testosterone and autistic traits. *British Journal of Psychology, 100*(1), 1–22. doi.org/10.1348/000712608X311731

Bailey, L., Ellis, S. J., & McNeil, J. (2014). Suicide risk in the UK trans population and the role of gender transition in decreasing suicidal ideation and suicide attempt. *Mental Health Review Journal, 19*(4), 209–220. doi.org/10.1108/MHRJ-05-2014-0015

Baird, G., Simonoff, E., Pickles, A., Chandler, S., Loucas, T., Meldrum, D., & Charman, T. (2006). Prevalence of disorders of the autism spectrum in a population cohort of children in South Thames: the Special Needs and Autism Project (SNAP). *The Lancet, 368*(9531), 210–215. doi.org/10.1016/S0140-6736(06)69041-7

Baker, K. E., Wilson, L. M., Sharma, R., Dukhanin, V., McArthur, K., & Robinson, K. A. (2021). Hormone therapy, mental health, and quality of life among transgender people: a systematic review. *Journal of the Endocrine Society, 5*(4), bvab011.

Barker, M. J., & Iantaffi, A. (2017). Psychotherapy. In C. Richard & W. P. Bouman (Eds.), *Genderqueer and non-binary genders* (pp. 103–124). London: Palgrave Macmillan.

Baron, D. (2018, September 4). A brief history of singular 'they'. *Oxford English Dictionary.* public.oed.com/blog/a-brief-history-of-singular-they/

Baron-Cohen, S. (2002). The extreme male brain theory of autism. *Trends in Cognitive Sciences, 6*(6), 248–254. doi.org/10.1016/S1364-6613(02)01904-6

Baron-Cohen, S., Richler, J., Bisarya, D., Gurunathan, N., & Wheelwright, S. (2003). The systemizing quotient: an investigation of adults with Asperger syndrome or high–functioning autism, and normal sex differences. *Philosophical Transactions of the Royal Society of London. Series B: Biological Sciences, 358*(1430), 361–374. doi.org /10.1098/rstb.2002.1206

Bauer, G. R., Lawson, M. L., & Metzger, D. L. (2022). Do clinical data from transgender adolescents support the phenomenon of 'rapid onset gender dysphoria'? *The Journal of Pediatrics, 243,* 224–227. e2. doi.org/10.1016/j.jpeds.2021.11.020

Beattie, M., & Evans, T. (2011). Holding breath: An analysis of gay men's schooldays memories. *Psychology of Sexualities Review, 2*(1), 10–24.

Begun, S., & Kattari, S. K. (2016). Conforming for survival: Associations between trans-gender visual conformity/passing and homelessness experiences. *Journal of Gay & Lesbian Social Services, 28*(1), 54–66. doi.org/10.1080/10538720.2016.1125821

Bellringer, J. (2017). Surgery for bodies commonly gendered as male. In C. Richards, W. P. Bouman, & M-J. Barker (Eds.), *Genderqueer and non-binary genders* (pp. 247–263). London: Palgrave Macmillan. doi.org/10.1057/978-1-137-51053-2_12

Betz, N. E., & Fitzgerald, L. F. (1993). Individuality and diversity: Theory and research in counseling psychology. *Annual Review of Psychology, 44*(1), 343–381. doi.org/10.1146 /annurev.ps.44.020193.002015

Billard, T. J. (2019). 'Passing' and the politics of deception: Transgender bodies, cisgen-der aesthetics, and the policing of inconspicuous marginal identities. In T. Docan-Morgan (Ed.), *The Palgrave handbook of deceptive communication* (pp. 463–477). Cham, Switzerland: Springer International Publishing. doi.org/10.1007/978-3-319-96334-1_24

binaohan, b. (2014). *Decolonizing trans gender 101*. Online: Biyuti Publishing.

Blackless, M., Charuvastra, A., Derryck, A., Fausto-Sterling, A., Lauzanne, K., & Lee, E. (2000). How sexually dimorphic are we? Review and synthesis. *American Journal of Human Biology: The Official Journal of the Human Biology Association, 12*(2), 151–166.

Blanchard, R. (1989). The classification and labeling of nonhomosexual gender dyspho-rias. *Archives of Sexual Behavior, 18*(4), 315–334. doi.org/10.1007/BF01541951

Boase, J. (2006). *The strength of internet ties.* www.pewinternet.org/pdfs/PIP_Internet_ ties.pdf

Bockting, W., Coleman, E., Deutsch, M. B., Guillamon, A., Meyer, I., Meyer, W., Reisner, S., Sevelius, J., & Ettner, R. (2016). Adult development and quality of life of transgen-der and gender nonconforming people. *Current Opinion in Endocrinology & Diabetes and Obesity, 23*(2), 188–197. doi.org/10.1097/MED.0000000000000232

Bockting, W. O., Miner, M. H., Swinburne Romine, R. E., Dolezal, C., Robinson, B. 'Bean' E., Rosser, B. R. S., & Coleman, E. (2020). The transgender identity survey: A measure of internalized transphobia. *LGBT Health, 7*(1), 15–27. doi.org/10.1089/lgbt.2018.0265

Bogaert, A. F. (2004). Asexuality: Prevalence and associated factors in a national proba-bility sample. *The Journal of Sex Research, 41*(3), 279–287. doi.org/10.1080/00224490 409552235

Bornstein, K. (2013). *My new gender workbook: A step-by-step guide to achieving world peace through gender anarchy and sex positivity.* London: Routledge.

Bouman, W. P., Claes, L., Brewin, N., Crawford, J. R., Millet, N., Fernandez-Aranda, F., & Arcelus, J. (2017). Transgender and anxiety: A comparative study between transgen-der people and the general population. *International Journal of Transgenderism, 18*(1), 16–26. doi.org/10.1080/15532739.2016.1258352

Brugha, T. S., McManus, S., Bankart, J., Scott, F., Purdon, S., Smith, J., … Meltzer, H. (2011). Epidemiology of autism spectrum disorders in adults in the community in England. *Archives of General Psychiatry, 68*(5), 459. doi.org/10.1001/archgenpsychiatry .2011.38

Budge, S. L., Adelson, J. L., & Howard, K. A. S. (2013). Anxiety and depression in transgender individuals: The roles of transition status, loss, social support, and coping. *Journal of Consulting and Clinical Psychology, 81*(3), 545–557. doi.org/10.1037/a0031774

Budge, S. L., Rossman, H. K., & Howard, K. A. (2014). Coping and psychological distress among genderqueer individuals: The moderating effect of social support. *Journal of LGBT Issues in Counseling, 8*(1), 95–117.

Buxton, A. P. (2006). When a spouse comes out: Impact on the heterosexual partner. *Sexual Addiction & Compulsivity, 13*(2–3), 317–332. doi.org/10.1080/10720160600897599

Clements-Nolle, K., Marx, R., Guzman, R., & Katz, M. (2001). HIV prevalence, risk behaviors, health care use, and mental health status of transgender persons: implications for public health intervention. *American Journal of Public Health, 91*(6), 915–921. doi.org/10.2105/AJPH.91.6.915

Clements-Nolle, K., Marx, R., & Katz, M. (2006). Attempted suicide among transgender persons. *Journal of Homosexuality, 51*(3), 53–69. doi.org/10.1300/J082v51n03_04

Coleman, E., Bockting, W., Botzer, M., Cohen-Kettenis, P., DeCuypere, G., Feldman, J., … Zucker, K. (2012). Standards of care for the health of transsexual, transgender, and gender-nonconforming people, Version 7. *International Journal of Transgenderism, 13*(4), 165–232. doi.org/10.1080/15532739.2011.700873

Coolhart, D., Ritenour, K., & Grodzinski, A. (2018). Experiences of ambiguous loss for parents of transgender male youth: A phenomenological exploration. *Contemporary Family Therapy, 40*(1), 28–41. doi.org/10.1007/s10591-017-9426-x

Craig, A. D. B. (2010). The sentient self. *Brain Structure and Function, 214*(5), 563–577. doi.org/10.1007/S00429-010-0248-Y

Crenshaw, K. (1989). Demarginalizing the intersection of race and sex: A Black feminist critique of antidiscrimination doctrine, feminist theory and antiracist politics. *University of Chicago Legal Forum, 1989*(8), 139–167. chicagounbound.uchicago.edu/uclf/vol1989/iss1/8

Damasio, A. (2003). Feelings of emotion and the self. *Annals of the New York Academy of Sciences, 1001*(1), 253–261. doi.org/10.1196/ANNALS.1279.014

Danker, S., Narayan, S. K., Bluebond-Langner, R., Schechter, L. S., & Berli, J. U. (2018). Abstract. *Plastic and Reconstructive Surgery – Global Open, 6*(9S), 189. doi.org/10.1097/01.GOX.0000547077.23299.00

Daskalos, C. T. (1998). Changes in the sexual orientation of six heterosexual male-to-female transsexuals. *Archives of Sexual Behavior, 27*(6), 605–614. doi.org/10.1023/A:1018725201811

Dave, S. S. (2003). Male circumcision in Britain: findings from a national probability sample survey. *Sexually Transmitted Infections, 79*(6), 499–500. doi.org/10.1136/sti.79.6.499

Davidmann, S. (2014). Imag(in)ing trans partnerships: Collaborative photography and intimacy. *Journal of Homosexuality, 61*(5), 636–653. doi.org/10.1080/00918369.2014.865481

Davies, S., McIntyre, S., & Rypma, C. (2019). *Detransition rates in a national UK gender identity clinic.* Poster.

de Graaf, N. M., Huisman, B., Cohen-Kettenis, P. T., Twist, J., Hage, K., Carmichael, P., … & Steensma, T. D. (2021). Psychological functioning in non-binary identifying adolescents and adults. *Journal of Sex & Marital Therapy, 47*(8), 773–84. www.tandfonline.com/doi/full/10.1080/0092623X.2021.1950087

Defreyne, J., Motmans, J., & T'sjoen, G. (2017). Healthcare costs and quality of life outcomes following gender affirming surgery in trans men: a review. *Expert Review of Pharmacoeconomics & Outcomes Research, 17*(6), 543–556. doi.org/10.1080/14737167.2017.1388164

Dhejne, C., Öberg, K., Arver, S., & Landén, M. (2014). An analysis of all applications for sex reassignment surgery in Sweden, 1960–2010: Prevalence, incidence, and regrets. *Archives of Sexual Behavior, 43*(8), 1535–1545. doi.org/10.1007/s10508-014-0300-8

Dhejne, C., van Vlerken, R., Heylens, G., & Arcelus, J. (2016). Mental health and gender dysphoria: A review of the literature. *International Review of Psychiatry, 28*(1), 44–57. doi.org/10.3109/09540261.2015.1115753

Downs, A. (2005). *The velvet rage: overcoming the pain of growing up gay in a straight man's world.* Boston: Da Capo Lifelong Books. http://proxy.lib.umich.edu/login? url= http://search.ebscohost.com/login.aspx?direct=true&db=qth&AN=57576079 &site= ehost-live&scope=site

Duby, Z., Nkosi, B., Scheibe, A., Brown, B., & Bekker, L. G. (2018). 'Scared of going to the clinic': Contextualising healthcare access for men who have sex with men, female sex workers and people who use drugs in two South African cities. *Southern African Journal of HIV Medicine, 19*(1). doi.org/10.4102/SAJHIVMED.V19I1.701

Eccles, J. S., Jacobs, J. E., & Harold, R. D. (1990). Gender role stereotypes, expectancy effects, and parents' socialization of gender differences. *Journal of Social Issues, 46*(2), 183–201. doi.org/10.1111/j.1540-4560.1990.tb01929.x

Evans, L., Scarrone Bonhomme, L., Seal, L., Rypma, C., & Richards, C. (2019, April). A comparison of the presenting issues and desired outcomes of people with a non-binary gender identity, between those assigned male at birth and those assigned female at birth at the UK Charing Cross NHS Gender Identity Clinic. *The 3rd Biennial European Professional Association for Transgender Health.*

Faccio, E., Bordin, E., & Cipolletta, S. (2013). Transsexual parenthood and new role assumptions. *Culture, Health & Sexuality, 15*(9), 1055–1070. doi.org/10.1080/13691058 .2013.806676

Fausto-Sterling, A. (2000). *Sexing the body: gender politics and the construction of sexuality* (1st ed.). New York: Basic Books.

Fausto-Sterling, A. (2012). *Sex/Gender: Biology in a Social World.* doi.org/10.4324 /9780203127971

Feder, S. (2020). *Disclosure: Trans lives on screen.* Film. www.researchgate.net/publication /362644148_Disclosure_Trans_Lives_on_Screen

Fitzgerald, T. J. (2010). Queerspawn and their families: Psychotherapy with LGBTQ families. *Journal of Gay and Lesbian Health, 14*(2), 155–162. doi.org/10.1080 /19359700903433276

Flores, A. (2020). *Two spirit and LGBTQ identities: Today and centuries ago.* Human Rights Campaign. www.hrc.org/news/two-spirit-and-lgbtq-idenitites-today-and-centuries -ago

Freedman, D., Tasker, F., & di Ceglie, D. (2002). Children and adolescents with transsexual parents referred to a specialist gender identity development service: A brief report of key developmental features. *Clinical Child Psychology and Psychiatry, 7*(3), 423–432. doi.org/10.1177/1359104502007003009

Frey, J. D., Poudrier, G., Chiodo, M. v., & Hazen, A. (2016). A systematic review of metoidioplasty and radial forearm flap phalloplasty in female-to-male transgender genital reconstruction. *Plastic and Reconstructive Surgery – Global Open, 4*(12), e1131. doi. org/10.1097/GOX.0000000000001131

Gagné, P., & Tewksbury, R. (1998). Conformity pressures and gender resistance among transgendered individuals. *Social Problems, 45*, 81–101.

Gallagher, S. (2005). How the body shapes the mind. In *Constructivist Foundations* (Vol. 5, Issue 2). Oxford University Press. proxy.libraries.smu.edu/login?url=http://search. ebscohost.com/login.aspx?direct=true&db=a9h&AN=51503537&site=ehost-live &scope=site

Galop. (2021). *Hate Crime Report*. galop.org.uk/wp-content/uploads/2021/06/Galop-Hate -Crime-Report-2021-1.pdf

George, R., & Stokes, M. A. (2018). A quantitative analysis of mental health among sexual and gender minority groups in ASD. *Journal of Autism and Developmental Disorders*, *48*(6), 2052–2063. doi.org/10.1007/s10803-018-3469-1

Gerhardstein, K. R. (2010). *Attitudes toward transsexual people: Effects of gender and appearance* [Indiana State University]. www.proquest.com/openview/ede7cf9699f-cf20f2f1f951226a4feb8/1?pq-origsite=gscholar&cbl=18750

Gilbert, P. (2009). *The compassionate mind*. London: Constable & Robinson.

Gilbert, P. (2010). *Compassion focused therapy: Distinctive features*. London: Taylor & Francis.

Gilbert, P. (2017). Compassion: Concepts, research and applications. In P. Gilbert (Ed.), *Compassion: Concepts, research and applications*. London: Routledge. doi.org/10 .4324/9781315564296

Gillespie, B. L., & Eisler, R. M. (1992). Development of the feminine gender role stress scale. *Behavior Modification*, *16*(3), 426–438. doi.org/10.1177/01454455920163008

Gilovich, T., Medvec, V. H., & Savitsky, K. (2000). The spotlight effect in social judgement: an egocentric bias in estimates of the salience of one's own actions and appearance. *Journal of Personality and Social Psychology*, *78*(2), 211.

Glidden, D., Bouman, W. P., Jones, B. A., & Arcelus, J. (2016). Gender dysphoria and autism spectrum disorder: A systematic review of the literature. *Sexual Medicine Reviews*, *4*(1), 3–14. doi.org/10.1016/j.sxmr.2015.10.003

Goldberg, A. E. (2010). *Lesbian and Gay Parents and Their Children: Research on the Family Life Cycle*. Washington, DC: American Psychological Association. doi.org/10 .1037/12055-000

Government Equalities Office. (2018). *National LGBT survey: Summmary report*. assets.publishing.service.gov.uk/government/uploads/system/uploads/attachment_ data/file/722314/GEO-LGBT-Survey-Report.pdf

Grant, J., Mottet, L., Tanis, J., Harrison, J., Herman, J., & Keisling, M. (2011). *Injustice at every turn: A report of the national transgender discrimination survey*. National Center for Transgender Equality and National Gay and Lesbian Task Force.

Green, J. (2020). *Becoming a visible man*. Nashville, TN: Vanderbilt University Press.

Greene, K., Derlega, V., & Mattews, A. (n.d.). Self-disclosure in personal relationships. In A. L. Vangelisti & D. Perlman (Eds.), *The Cambridge handbook of personal relationships* (pp. 409–427). Cambridge: Cambridge University Press.

Haines, B. A., Ajayi, A. A., & Boyd, H. (2014). Making trans parents visible: Intersectionality of trans and parenting identities. *Feminism & Psychology*, *24*(2), 238–247. doi. org/10.1177/0959353514526219

Hamilton, C. J., & Mahalik, J. R. (2009). Minority stress, masculinity, and social norms predicting gay men's health risk behaviors. *Journal of Counseling Psychology*, *56*(1), 132–141. doi.org/10.1037/a0014440

Haney-López, Ian. (1996). *White by law: the legal construction of race*. New York University Press.

Hepp, U., Kraemer, B., Schnyder, U., Miller, N., & Delsignore, A. (2005). Psychiatric comorbidity in gender identity disorder. *Journal of Psychosomatic Research*, *58*(3), 259–261. doi.org/10.1016/j.jpsychores.2004.08.010

Herman, J. (2016). LGB within the T: Sexual orientation in the national transgender discrimination survey and implications for public policy. In Y. Martinez-San Miguel & S. Tobias (Eds.), *Trans studies: The challenge to hetero/homo normativities, an interdisciplinary essay collection*. New Brunswick, NJ: Rutgers University Press. escholarship .org/uc/item/4n7727j7

Heylens, G., Aspeslagh, L., Dierickx, J., Baetens, K., van Hoorde, B., de Cuypere, G., & Elaut, E. (2018). The co-occurrence of gender dysphoria and autism spectrum disorder in adults: An analysis of cross-sectional and clinical chart data. *Journal of Autism and Developmental Disorders, 48*(6), 2217–2223. doi.org/10.1007/s10803-018-3480-6

Hilty, D. M., Ferrer, D. C., Parish, M. B., Johnston, B., Callahan, E. J., & Yellowlees, P. M. (2013). The effectiveness of telemental health: A 2013 review. *Telemedicine and e-Health, 19*(6), 444–454. doi.org/10.1089/TMJ.2013.0075

Hinchy, J. (2019). *Governing gender and sexuality in colonial India: The Hijra, c. 1850-1900*. Cambridge: Cambridge University Press.

Hines, S. (2006). Intimate transitions: Transgender practices of partnering and parenting. *Sociology, 40*(2), 353–371. doi.org/10.1177/0038038506062037

Hu, W., Lu, J., Zhang, L., Wu, W., Nie, H., Zhu, Y., ... & Bai, Y. (2006). A preliminary report of penile transplantation. *European Urology, 50*(4), 851–853. doi.org/10.1016/j.eururo.2006.07.026

Hunt, J. (2014). An initial study of transgender people's experiences of seeking and receiving counselling or psychotherapy in the UK. *Counselling and Psychotherapy Research, 14*(4), 288–296. doi.org/10.1080/14733145.2013.838597

Iantaffi, A., & Barker, M.-J. (2020). *Gender trauma: Healing cultural, social, and historical gendered trauma*. London: Jessica Kingsley Publishers.

Introcaso, C., Xu, F., Kilmarx, P., Zaidi, A., & Markowitx, L. E. (2013). Prevalence of circumcision among men and boys aged 14 to 59 years in the United States, National Health and Nutrition Examination Surveys 2005–2010. *Sexually Transmitted Diseases, 40*(7), 521–525. www.jstor.org/stable/48511607

Istarlev, A., & Sennott, S. (2012). Transsexual desire in differently gendered bodies. In J. J. Bigner & J. L. Wetchler (Eds.), *Handbook of LGBT-affirmative couple and family therapy*. New York: Routledge.

Jahromi, A. H., Horen, S. R., Dorafshar, A. H., Seu, M. L., Radix, A., Anderson, E., ... & Schechter, L. (2021). Uterine transplantation and donation in transgender individuals; proof of concept. *International Journal of Transgender Health, 22*(4), 1–11. doi.org/10.1080/26895269.2021.1915635

James, S., Herman, J., Rankin, S., Keisling, M., Mottet, L., & Anafi, M. (2016). *The Report of the 2015 U.S. Transgender Survey*. Washington, DC: National Center for Transgender Equality. transequality.org/sites/default/files/docs/usts/USTS-Full-Report-Dec17.pdf

Javier, C., Crimston, C. R., & Barlow, F. K. (2022). Surgical satisfaction and quality of life outcomes reported by transgender men and women at least one year post gender-affirming surgery: A systematic literature review. *International Journal of Transgender Health, 23*(3), 255–273. doi.org/10.1080/26895269.2022.2038334

Jenkin, E. (2022, February 7). *The Instagram effect*. BBC3 documentary. www.bbc.co.uk/programmes/m00149j7

Jiang, D., Witten, J., Berli, J., & Dugi, D. (2018). Does depth matter? Factors affecting choice of vulvoplasty over vaginoplasty as gender-affirming genital surgery for transgender women. *The Journal of Sexual Medicine, 15*(6), 902–906. doi.org/10.1016/j.jsxm.2018.03.085

Johnson, D. E. (2014). *The impact of microaggresions in therapy on transgender and gender-nonconforming clients: A concurrent nested design study*. University of the Rockies.

Jones, R. M., Wheelwright, S., Farrell, K., Martin, E., Green, R., di Ceglie, D., & Baron-Cohen, S. (2011). Brief report: Female-to-male transsexual people and autistic traits. *Journal of Autism and Developmental Disorders, 42*(2), 301–306. doi.org/10.1007/S10803-011-1227-8

Kaltiala-Heino, R., Sumia, M., Työläjärvi, M., & Lindberg, N. (2015). Two years of gender identity service for minors: Overrepresentation of natal girls with severe problems in adolescent development. *Child and Adolescent Psychiatry and Mental Health, 9*(1), 1–9. doi.org/10.1186/s13034-015-0042-y

Kattari, S. K., Walls, N. E., Whitfield, D. L., & Langenderfer-Magruder, L. (2015). Racial and ethnic differences in experiences of discrimination in accessing health services among transgender people in the United States. *International Journal of Transgenderism, 16*(2), 68–79. doi.org/10.1080/15532739.2015.1064336

Kennedy, J. (2008). The transgender movement. *Christianity Today, 52*(2), 54–58.

Kocsis, B. J., & Yellowlees, P. (2018). Telepsychotherapy and the therapeutic relationship: Principles, advantages, and case examples. *Telemedicine and e-Health, 24*(5), 329–334. doi.org/10.1089/TMJ.2017.0088

Koehler, A., Eyssel, J., & Nieder, T. O. (2018). Genders and individual treatment progress in (non-)binary trans individuals. *The Journal of Sexual Medicine, 15*(1), 102–113. doi.org/10.1016/j.jsxm.2017.11.007

Kolk, B. van der. (2015). *The body keeps the score: Mind, brain and body in the transformation of trauma.* London: Penguin Books.

Kotula, D. (2002). *The phallus palace: Female to male transsexuals* (1st ed.). Los Angeles: Alyson Publications.

Kristensen, Z. E., & Broome, M. R. (2015). Autistic traits in an internet sample of gender variant UK adults. *International Journal of Transgenderism, 16*(4), 234–245. doi.org/10.1080/15532739.2015.1094436

Kuper, L. E., Nussbaum, R., & Mustanski, B. (2012). Exploring the diversity of gender and sexual orientation identities in an online sample of transgender individuals. *The Journal of Sex Research, 49*(2–3), 244–254. doi.org/10.1080/00224499.2011.596954

Laird, J. (1996). Invisible ties: Lesbians and their families of origin. In J. Laird & R.-J. Green (Eds.), *Lesbians and gays in couples and families: A handbook for therapists* (pp. 89–122). San Francisco: Jossey-Bass Publishers. psycnet.apa.org/record/1996-98094-004

Lawrence, A. A. (2003). Factors associated with satisfaction or regret following male-to-female sex reassignment surgery. *Archives of Sexual Behavior, 32*(4), 299–315. doi.org/10.1023/A:1024086814364

Lawrence, A. A. (2005). Sexuality before and after male-to-female sex reassignment surgery. *Archives of Sexual Behavior, 34*(2), 147–166. doi.org/10.1007/s10508-005-1793-y

Lawrence, A. A. (2007). Becoming what we love: Autogynephilic transsexualism conceptualized as an expression of romantic love. *Perspectives in Biology and Medicine, 50*(4), 506. doi.org/10.1353/pbm.2007.0050

LeBreton, M., Courtois, F., Journel, N. M., Beaulieu-Prévost, D., Bélanger, M., Ruffion, A., & Terrier, J.-É. (2017). Genital sensory detection thresholds and patient satisfaction with vaginoplasty in male-to-female transgender women. *The Journal of Sexual Medicine, 14*(2), 274–281. doi.org/10.1016/j.jsxm.2016.12.005

Leon, A. [@alexand_erleon]. (2020, January 7). *Queer people don't grow up as ourselves, we grow up playing a version of ourselves that sacrifices authenticity to minimise [Tweet].* Twitter. twitter.com/alexand_erleon/status/1214459404575100928?lang=en

Leppel, K. (2016). The labor force status of transgender men and women. *International Journal of Transgenderism, 17*(3–4), 155–164. doi.org/10.1080/15532739.2016.1236312

Levy, D. L., & Lo, J. R. (2013). Transgender, transsexual, and gender queer individuals with a Christian upbringing: The process of resolving conflict between gender identity and faith. *Journal of Religion & Spirituality in Social Work: Social Thought, 32*(1), 60–83. doi.org/10.1080/15426432.2013.749079

Lewins, F. W. (1995). *Transsexualism in society: A sociology of male-to-female transsexuals.* South Melbourne, Victoria: Macmillan Education Australia.

Lin, C.-S., Ku, H.-L., Chao, H.-T., Tu, P.-C., Li, C.-T., Cheng, ... & Hsieh, J.-C. (2014). Neural network of body representation differs between transsexuals and cissexuals. *PLoS ONE, 9*(1), e85914. doi.org/10.1371/journal.pone.0085914

Loh, J. U. (2014). Narrating identity: The employment of mythological and literary narratives in identity formation among the Hijras of India. *Religion and Gender, 4*(1), 21–39.

López, A. J. (2005). *Postcolonial whiteness: A critical reader on race and empire.* State University of New York Press.

Lykens, J. E., LeBlanc, A. J., & Bockting, W. O. (2018). Healthcare experiences among young adults who identify as genderqueer or nonbinary. *LGBT Health, 5*(3), 191–196.

Maguen, S., & Shipherd, J. C. (2010). Suicide risk among transgender individuals. *Psychology and Sexuality, 1*(1), 34–43. doi.org/10.1080/19419891003634430

Mahalik, J. R., Morray, E. B., Coonerty-Femiano, A., Ludlow, L. H., Slattery, S. M., & Smiler, A. (2005). Development of the conformity to feminine norms inventory. *Sex Roles, 52*(7–8), 417–435. doi.org/10.1007/s11199-005-3709-7

Manrique, O. J., Adabi, K., Martinez-Jorge, J., Ciudad, P., Nicoli, F., & Kiranantawat, K. (2018). Complications and patient-reported outcomes in male-to-female vaginoplasty – where we are today. *Annals of Plastic Surgery, 80*(6), 684–691. doi.org/10.1097/SAP.0000000000001393

Markowe, L. (2006). Coming out as lesbian. In A. Coyle & C. C. Kitzinger (Eds.), *Lesbian and gay psychology: New perspectives* (pp. 66–80). British Psychological Society.

Marotta, B. (2017). *American Circumcision.* [film]

Marshall, K. (2020). *The gender binary is a tool of white supremacy.* Medium. aninjusticemag.com/the-gender-binary-is-a-tool-of-white-supremacy-db89d0bc9044

Matsuno, E., & Budge, S. L. (2017). Non-binary/genderqueer identities: A critical review of the literature. *Current Sexual Health Reports, 9*, 116–120.

McDermott, R. C., Levant, R. F., Hammer, J. H., Borgogna, N. C., & McKelvey, D. K. (2019). Development and validation of a five-item Male Role Norms Inventory using bifactor modeling. *Psychology of Men & Masculinities, 20*(4), 467–477. doi.org/10.1037/men0000178

McDermott, R. C., Wolfe, G., Levant, R. F., Alshabani, N., & Richmond, K. (2021). Measurement invariance of three gender ideology scales across cis, trans, and nonbinary gender identities. *Psychology of Men & Masculinities, 22*(2), 331–344. doi.org/10.1037/men0000286

McGuire, J. K., Catalpa, J. M., Lacey, V., & Kuvalanka, K. A. (2016). Ambiguous loss as a framework for interpreting gender transitions in families. *Journal of Family Theory & Review, 8*(3), 373–385. doi.org/10.1111/jftr.12159

Menvielle, E. J., & Rodnan, L. A. (2011). A therapeutic group for parents of transgender adolescents. *Child and Adolescent Psychiatric Clinics of North America, 20*(4), 733–743. doi.org/10.1016/j.chc.2011.08.002

Merleau-Ponty, M. (1964). The child's reaction with others. In M. Merleau-Ponty (Ed.), *The primacy of perception* (pp. 96–155). Evanston, Ill: Northwestern University Press.

Messinger, A. M., Guadalupe-Diaz, X. L., & Kurdyla, V. (2021). Transgender polyvictimization in the U.S. Transgender Survey. doi.org/10.1177/08862605211039250

Meyer, I. H. (1995). Minority stress and mental health in gay men. *Journal of Health and Social Behavior, 36*(1), 38. doi.org/10.2307/2137286

Millet, N., Longworth, J., & Arcelus, J. (2017). Prevalence of anxiety symptoms and disorders in the transgender population: A systematic review of the literature. *International Journal of Transgenderism, 18*(1), 27–38. doi.org/10.1080/15532739.2016.1258353

Minkin, R., & Brown, A. (2021). *Rising shares of U.S. adults know someone who is transgender or goes by gender-neutral pronouns.* www.pewresearch.org/fact-tank /2021/07/27/rising-shares-of-u-s-adults-know-someone-who-is-transgender-or-goes -by-gender-neutral-pronouns/

Minosh, K. (2016, July 21). *Why non-natives appropriating "Two-spirit" hurts.* BGD. www.bgdblog.org/2016/07/appropriating-two-spirit/

Moradi, B., Mohr, J. J., Worthington, R. L., & Fassinger, R. E. (2009). Counseling psychology research on sexual (orientation) minority issues: Conceptual and methodological challenges and opportunities. *Journal of Counseling Psychology, 56*(1), 5–22. doi .org/10.1037/a0014572

Morris, B. J., Bailis, S. A., & Wiswell, T. E. (2014). Circumcision rates in the United States: Rising or falling? What effect might the new affirmative pediatric policy statement have? *Mayo Clinic Proceedings, 89*(5), 677–686. doi.org/10.1016/j.mayocp.2014.01.001

Moser, C. (2009). Autogynephilia in women. *Journal of Homosexuality, 56*(5), 539–547. doi.org/10.1080/00918360903005212

Moser, C. (2010). Blanchard's autogynephilia theory: A critique. *Journal of Homosexuality, 57*(6), 790–809. doi.org/10.1080/00918369.2010.486241

Motmans, J., Dierckx, M., & Mortelmans, D. (2018). Transgender families. In W. Bouman & J. Arcelus (Eds.), *The transgender handbook: A guide for transgender people, their families and professionals.* New York: Nova Science Publishers.

Moye, L. (2018). Transgender and gender non-conforming clients' experiences in therapy, working alliance, and the letter of transition [William James College]. In *William James College ProQuest Dissertations Publishing.* www.proquest.com/openview/22aaf-6b57aa9e7c73eadbec89d88b0c0/1?pq-origsite=gscholar&cbl=18750&diss=y

Mueller, S. C., de Cuypere, G., & T'Sjoen, G. (2017). Transgender research in the 21st century: A selective critical review from a neurocognitive perspective. *American Journal of Psychiatry, 174*(12), 1155–1162. doi.org/10.1176/appi.ajp.2017.17060626

Najmabadi, A. (2001). Gendered transformations: Beauty, love, and sexuality in Qajar Iran. *Iranian Studies, 34*(1–4), 89–102. doi.org/10.1080/00210860108701998

Newfield, E., Hart, S., Dibble, S., & Kohler, L. (2006). Female-to-male transgender quality of life. *Quality of Life Research, 15*(9), 1447–1457. doi.org/10.1007/s11136-006-0002-3

NHS. (2020, May 28). *Treatment. Gender Dysphoria.* Treatment. Gender dysphoria. www.nhs.uk/conditions/gender-dysphoria/treatment/

Nonbinary.wiki. (n.d.). Retrieved August 19, 2022, nonbinary.wiki/wiki/Main_Page

Norwood, K. (2013). Grieving gender: Trans-identities, transition, and ambiguous loss. *Communication Monographs, 80*(1), 24–45. doi.org/10.1080/03637751.2012.739705

Ntumy, M., Maya, E., Lizneva, D., Adanu, R., & Azziz, R. (2019). The pressing need for standardization in epidemiologic studies of PCOS across the globe. *Gynecological Endocrinology, 35*(1), 1–3. doi.org/10.1080/09513590.2018.1488958

Nuttbrock, L., Hwahng, S., Bockting, W., Rosenblum, A., Mason, M., Macri, M., & Becker, J. (2010). Psychiatric impact of gender-related abuse across the life course of male-to-female transgender persons. *Journal of Sex Research, 47*(1), 12–23. doi.org/10.1080 /00224490903062258

Nuttbrock, L., Rosenblum, A., & Blumenstein, R. (2002). Transgender identity affirmation and mental health. *International Journal of Transgenderism, 6*(4).

Olson, K. R., Durwood, L., Demeules, M., & McLaughlin, K. A. (2016). Mental health of transgender children who are supported in their identities. *Pediatrics, 137*(3). doi. org/10.1542/peds.2015-3223

O'Neil, J. M. (1981). Male sex role conflicts, sexism, and masculinity: Psychological implications for men, women, and the counseling psychologist. *The Counseling Psychologist, 9*(2), 61–80. doi.org/10.1177/001100008100900213

O'Neil, J. M. (2008). Summarizing 25 years of research on men's gender role conflict using the gender role conflict scale. *The Counseling Psychologist, 36*(3), 358–445. doi.org/10.1177/0011000008317057

O'Neil, J. M., Helms, B. J., Gable, R. K., David, L., & Wrightsman, L. S. (1986). Gender-role conflict scale: College men's fear of femininity. *Sex Roles, 14*(5–6), 335–350. doi. org/10.1007/BF00287583

Orlowski-Yang, J. (2020). *The Social Dilemma.* Netflix.

PACE. (2015). *The RaRE Research Report: LGB&T mental health – risk and resilience explored.* www.queerfutures.co.uk/wp-content/uploads/2015/04/RARE_Research_Report_ PACE_2015.pdf

Papadopulos, N. A., Ehrenberger, B., Zavlin, D., Lellé, J.-D., Henrich, G., Kovacs, L., ... & Schaff, J. (2021). Quality of life and satisfaction in transgender men after phalloplasty in a retrospective study. *Annals of Plastic Surgery, 87*(1), 91–97. doi.org/10.1097 /SAP.0000000000002693

Pasterski, V., Gilligan, L., & Curtis, R. (2014). Traits of autism spectrum disorders in adults with gender dysphoria. *Archives of Sexual Behavior, 43*(2), 387–393. doi.org/10 .1007/s10508-013-0154-5

Pearlman, S. F. (2006). Terms of connection. *Journal of GLBT Family Studies, 2*(3–4), 93–122. doi.org/10.1300/J461v02n03_06

Pfeffer, C. A. (2014). 'I don't like passing as a straight woman': Queer negotiations of identity and social group membership. *American Journal of Sociology, 120*(1), 1–44. doi.org/10.1086/677197

Pipkin, A. (2021). The psychological needs of people with non-binary gender identities. *Clinical Psychology Forum, 339*, 24–28.

Porges, S. (2011). *The polyvagal theory: Neurophysiological foundations of emotions, attachment communication, self-regulation.* New York: Norton.

PornHub. (2019, December 11). *The 2019 year in review.* www.pornhub.com/insights /2019-year-in-review

Pulver, M. (1999). *Tribut der Seuche oder: Seuchenmythen als Quelle sozialer Kallibrierung.* New York: Peter Lang Publishing.

Ralph, D., Christopher, N., & Garaffa, G. (2017). Genital surgery for bodies commonly gendered as female. In *Genderqueer and Non-Binary Genders* (pp. 265–282). London: Palgrave Macmillan. doi.org/10.1057/978-1-137-51053-2_13

Richmond, K., Levant, R., Smalley, B., & Cook, S. (2015). The femininity ideology scale (FIS): Dimensions and its relationship to anxiety and feminine gender role stress. *Women & Health, 55*(3), 263–279. doi.org/10.1080/03630242.2014.996723

Riggs, D. W., & Bartholomaeus, C. (2018). Cisgenderism and certitude: Parents of transgender children negotiating educational contexts. *TSQ: Transgender Studies Quarterly, 5*(1), 67–82. doi.org/10.1215/23289252-4291529

Riggs, D. W., Fraser, H., Taylor, N., Signal, T., & Donovan, C. (2016). Domestic violence service providers' capacity for supporting transgender women: Findings from an Australian workshop. *British Journal of Social Work, 46*(8), 2374–2392. doi.org/10. 1093/bjsw/bcw110

Rimes, K. A., Goodship, N., Ussher, G., Baker, D., & West, E. (2019). Non-binary and binary transgender youth: Comparison of mental health, self-harm, suicidality, substance use and victimization experiences. *International Journal of Transgenderism, 20*(2–3), 230–240. doi.org/10.1080/15532739.2017.1370627

Rogers, M. (2017). Transphobic 'honour'-based abuse: A conceptual tool. *Sociology, 51*(2), 225–240. doi.org/10.1177/0038038515622907

Rosser, B. R. S., Bockting, W. O., Ross, M. W., Miner, M. H., & Coleman, E. (2008). The relationship between homosexuality, internalized homo-negativity, and mental health in men who have sex with men. *Journal of Homosexuality, 55*(2), 185–203. doi.org/10.1080/00918360802129394

Rotondi, N. K., Bauer, G. R., Scanlon, K., Kaay, M., Travers, R., & Travers, A. (2011). Prevalence of and risk and protective factors for depression in female-to-male transgender Ontarians: Trans PULSE project. *Canadian Journal of Community Mental Health, 30*(2), 135–155. doi.org/10.7870/cjcmh-2011-0021

Salari, N., Hosseinian-Far, A., Jalali, R., Vaisi-Raygani, A., Rasoulpoor, S., Mohammadi, M., ... & Khaledi-Paveh, B. (2020). Prevalence of stress, anxiety, depression among the general population during the COVID-19 pandemic: A systematic review and meta-analysis. *Globalization and Health, 16*(1), 1–11. doi.org/10.1186/s12992-020-00589-w

Sánchez, F. J., & Vilain, E. (2009). Collective self-esteem as a coping resource for male-to-female transsexuals. *Journal of Counseling Psychology, 56*(1), 202–209. doi.org/10.1037/a0014573

Sánchez, M. C., & Schlossberg, L. (2001). *Passing: Identity and interpretation in sexuality, race, and religion.* New York University Press.

Sanderson, C. (2013). *Counselling skills for working with trauma: Healing from child sex abuse, sexual violence and domestic abuse.* London: Jessica Kingsley.

Sanger, T. (2010). *Trans people's partnerships: Towards an ethics of intimacy.* New York: Palgrave Macmillan.

Savin-Williams, R. (1996). Self-labelling and disclosure among gay, lesbian and bisexual youth. In J. Laird & R. J. Green (Eds.), *Lesbians and gays in couples and families* (pp. 153–182). San Francisco: Jossey-Bass Publishers.

Sax, L. (2002). How common is intersex? A response to Anne Fausto-Sterling. *The Journal of Sex Research, 39*(3), 174–178. doi.org/10.1080/00224490209552139

Scandurra, C., Mezza, F., Maldonato, N. M., Bottone, M., Bochicchio, V., Valerio, P., & Vitelli, R. (2019). Health of non-binary and genderqueer people: A systematic review. *Frontiers in Psychology, 10.* doi.org/10.3389/fpsyg.2019.01453

Scarrone Bonhomme, L. (2019a). Gender dysphoria and the mirror: A mediator between the first person and the third person perspective. *Counselling Psychology Review, 34*(1), 51–59.

Scarrone Bonhomme, L. (2019b, September 17). Understanding and overcoming identity based trauma. *Trauma: Triggers, treatment and transformation: A multi-disciplinary exploration of trauma.*

Scarrone Bonhomme, L. (2021). The age of rediscovery: What it's like to gender transition when you are 50+. In T. Hafford-Letchfield, P. Reynolds, & P. Simpson (Eds.), *Sex and diversity in later life: Critical perspectives.* Bristol University Press.

Schardein, J. N., & Nikolavsky, D. (2022). Sexual functioning of transgender females post-vaginoplasty: Evaluation, outcomes and treatment strategies for sexual dysfunction. *Sexual Medicine Reviews, 10*(1), 77–90. doi.org/10.1016/j.sxmr.2021.04.001

Seal, L. (2017). Adult endocrinology. In C. Richards, W. P. Bouman, & M.-J. Barker (Eds.), *Genderqueer and non-binary genders* (pp. 183–223). London: Palgrave Macmillan. doi.org/10.1057/978-1-137-51053-2_10

Sequeira, G. M., Chakraborti, C., & Panunti, B. A. (2012). Integrating lesbian, gay, bisexual, and transgender (LGBT) content into undergraduate medical school curricula: A qualitative study. *Ochsner Journal, 12*(4).

Serano, J. (2007). *Whipping girl: A transsexual woman on sexism and the scapegoating of femininity.* New York: Seal Press.

Serano, J. (2020). Autogynephilia: A scientific review, feminist analysis, and alternative 'embodiment fantasies' model. *The Sociological Review, 68*(4), 763–778. doi.org/10.1177/0038026120934690

Shadyac, T. (1994). *Ace Ventura: Pet Detective.* [film]

Shapiro, E. (2004). 'Trans' cending Barriers. *Journal of Gay & Lesbian Social Services*, *16*(3–4), 165–179. doi.org/10.1300/J041v16n03_11

Shoptaw, S., Weiss, R. E., Munjas, B., Hucks-Ortiz, C., Young, S. D., Larkins, S., ... & Gorbach, P. M. (2009). Homonegativity, substance use, sexual risk behaviors, and HIV status in poor and ethnic men who have sex with men in Los Angeles. *Journal of Urban Health*, *86*(SUPPL. 1), 77–92. dx.doi.org/10.1007/s11524-009-9372-5

Singh, A. A., Hays, D. G., & Watson, L. S. (2011). Strength in the face of adversity: Resilience strategies of transgender individuals. *Journal of Counseling & Development*, *89*(1), 20–27. doi.org/10.1002/j.1556-6678.2011.tb00057.x

Singh, A. A., & McKleroy, V. S. (2011). "Just getting out of bed is a revolutionary act": The resilience of transgender people of color who have survived traumatic life events. *Traumatology*, *17*(2), 34–44. doi.org/10.1177/1534765610369261

Stolakis, K. (2021, June 16). *Pray away*. [Documentary] Netflix.

Stone, K. (2007). 'Do not be conformed to this world': Queer reading and the task of the preacher. *Theology & Sexuality*, *13*(2), 153–165. doi.org/10.1177/13558 35806074431

Stonewall. (2017a). *LGBT in Britain. Hate crime and discrimination*. www.stonewall. org.uk/system/files/lgbt_in_britain_hate_crime.pdf

Stonewall. (2017b). *The school report*. www.stonewall.org.uk/school-report-2017

Stroumsa, D. (2014). The state of transgender health care: Policy, law, and medical frameworks. *American Journal of Public Health*, *104*(3), e31–e38. doi.org/10.2105 /AJPH.2013.301789

Takizawa, R., Maughan, B., & Arseneault, L. (2014). Adult health outcomes of childhood bullying victimization: Evidence from a five-decade longitudinal British birth cohort. *American Journal of Psychiatry*, *171*(7), 777–784. doi.org/10.1176/appi.ajp.2014 .13101401

Testa, R. J., Jimenez, C. L., & Rankin, S. (2014). Risk and resilience during transgender identity development: The effects of awareness and engagement with other transgender people on affect. *Journal of Gay & Lesbian Mental Health*, *18*(1), 31–46. doi.org /10.1080/19359705.2013.805177

Testoni, I., & Pinducciu, M. A. (2019). Grieving those who still live: Loss experienced by parents of transgender children. *Gender Studies*, *18*(1), 142–162. doi.org/10.2478 /genst-2020-0011

TGEU. (2022, April 6). *Czech Court maintains mandatory sterilisation for LGR. Legal Gender Recognition*. tgeu.org/czech-court-maintains-mandatory-sterilisation-for-lgr/

The Trevor Project. (2022). *Diversity of nonbinary youth*. www.thetrevorproject.org /research-briefs/diversity-of-nonbinary-youth/

Towle, E. B., & Morgan, L. M. (2006). Romancing the transgender native: Rethinking the use of the 'third gender' concept. In S. Stryker & S. Whittle (Eds.), *The transgender studies reader* (pp. 666–684). London: Routledge.

Tuite, J., Rubenstein, L. D., & Salloum, S. J. (2021). The coming out experiences of gifted, LGBTQ students: When, to whom, and why not? *Journal for the Education of the Gifted*, *44*(4), 366–397. doi.org/10.1177/01623532211044538

Turban, J. L., King, D., Reisner, S. L., & Keuroghlian, A. S. (2019). Psychological attempts to change a person's gender identity from transgender to cisgender: Estimated prevalence across US states, 2015. *American Journal of Public Health*, *109*(10), 1452–1454. doi.org/10.2105/AJPH.2019.305237

Twist, J. (2017). Transitioning together: Narratives of sexuality and intimacy. *Psychology of Sexualities Review*, *8*(2), 77–92.

UK Trauma Council. (2022, July 30). *Definition of trauma*. uktraumacouncil.org/trauma /trauma?cn-reloaded=1)

Vanderburgh, Reid. (2007). *Transition and beyond: Observation on gender identity.* Portland, Oregon: Q Press.

Veale, J. F. (2015). Comments on ethical reporting and interpretations of findings in Hsu, Rosenthal, and Bailey's (2014) 'The psychometric structure of items assessing autogynephilia'. *Archives of Sexual Behavior, 44*(7), 1743–1746. doi.org/10.1007/s10508-015 -0552-y

Veale, J. F., Clarke, D. E., & Lomax, T. C. (2008). Sexuality of Male-to-Female Transsexuals. *Archives of Sexual Behavior, 37*(4), 586–597. doi.org/10.1007/s10508-007-9306-9

Vincent, B. (2019). Breaking down barriers and binaries in trans healthcare: the validation of non-binary people. *International Journal of Transgenderism, 20*(2–3), 132–137. doi.org/10.1080/15532739.2018.1534075

Walsh, R. J., Krabbendam, L., Dewinter, J., & Begeer, S. (2018). Brief report: Gender identity differences in autistic adults: Associations with perceptual and socio-cognitive profiles. *Journal of Autism and Developmental Disorders, 48*(12), 4070–4078. doi.org/10 .1007/s10803-018-3702-y

Weber, G. (2008). Using to numb the pain: Substance use and abuse among lesbian, gay, and bisexual individuals. *Journal of Mental Health Counseling, 30*(1), 31–48. doi.org/10 .17744/mehc.30.1.2585916185422570

Weisgram, E. S., & Bruun, S. T. (2018). Predictors of gender-typed toy purchases by prospective parents and mothers: The roles of childhood experiences and gender attitudes. *Sex Roles, 79*(5–6), 342–357. doi.org/10.1007/s11199-018-0928-2

White, T., & Ettner, R. (2004). Disclosure, risks and protective factors for children whose parents are undergoing a gender transition. *Journal of Gay and Lesbian Psychotherapy, 8*(1–2), 129–145. psycnet.apa.org/record/2004-19367-010

White, T., & Ettner, R. (2007). Adaptation and adjustment in children of transsexual parents. *European Child & Adolescent Psychiatry, 16*(4), 215–221. doi.org/10.1007 /s00787-006-0591-y

Wiepjes, C. M., Nota, N. M., de Blok, C. J. M., Klaver, M., de Vries, A. L. C., Wensing-Kruger, S. A., ... & den Heijer, M. (2018). The Amsterdam cohort of gender dysphoria study (1972–2015): Trends in prevalence, treatment, and regrets. *The Journal of Sexual Medicine, 15*(4), 582–590. doi.org/10.1016/j.jsxm.2018.01.016

Wilcox, M. M. (2002). When Sheila's a lesbian: Religious individualism among lesbian, gay, bisexual, and transgender Christians. *Sociology of Religion, 63*(4), 497. doi.org/10 .2307/3712304

Wolke, D., & Lereya, S. T. (2015). Long-term effects of bullying. *Archives of Disease in Childhood, 100*(9), 879–885. doi.org/10.1136/archdischild-2014-306667

Wollrad, E. (2005). *Weisssein im widerspruch: feministische perspektiven auf rassismus, kultur und religion.* Königstein/Taunus, Germany: Helmer.

World Health Organization. (1992). *The ICD-10 classification of mental and behavioural disorders: clinical descriptions and diagnostic guidelines.*

World Health Organization. (2014). *Preventing suicide: A global imperative.* www.who.int

Yalom, I. (2015). *Creatures of a day: and other tales of psychotherapy.* New York: Basic Books.

Young, E. (2020). *They/them/their: A guide to nonbinary and genderqueer identities.* London: Jessica Kingsley Publishers.

Zamperini, A., Testoni, I., Primo, D., & Prandelli, M. (2016). Because moms say so: Narratives of lesbian mothers in Italy. *Journal of GLBT Family Studies, 12*(1), 91–110. doi.org/10.1080/1550428X.2015.1102669

Zavlin, D., Schaff, J., Lellé, J.-D., Jubbal, K. T., Herschbach, P., Henrich, G., ... & Papadopulos, N. A. (2018). Male-to-female sex reassignment surgery using the combined vaginoplasty technique: Satisfaction of transgender patients with aesthetic, functional, and sexual outcomes. *Aesthetic Plastic Surgery*, *42*(1), 178–187. doi.org/10.1007/s00266 -017-1003-z

Zhang, Q., Goodman, M., Adams, N., Corneil, T., Hashemi, L., Kreukels, B., ... & Coleman, E. (2020). Epidemiological considerations in transgender health: A systematic review with focus on higher quality data. *International Journal of Transgender Health*, *21*(2), 125–137. doi.org/10.1080/26895269.2020.1753136

Zhou, J.-N., Hofman, M. A., Gooren, L. J. G., & Swaab, D. F. (1995). A sex difference in the human brain and its relation to transsexuality. *Nature*, *378*(6552), 68–70. doi.org/10 .1038/378068a0

Index